EVERY CHILD NEEDS A MENTOR

HERMAN STEWART

Every Child Needs a Mentor

First published in 2012 by
Ecademy Press
48 St Vincent Drive, St Albans, Herts, AL1 5SJ
info@ecademy-press.com
www.ecademy-press.com

Printed and bound by Lightning Source in the UK and USA.
Cover Designed by Marianne Hartley.
Cover Photography by Ingrid Marn.
Text layout by Neil Coe.
Pre-editing by Joanne-Benjamin Lewis.

Printed on acid-free paper from managed forests. This book is printed on demand, so no copies will be remaindered or pulped.

ISBN 978-1-908746-06-1

The right of Herman Stewart to be identified as the author of this work has been inserted in accordance with sections 77 and 78 of the Copyright Designs and Patents Act 1988.

A CIP catalogue record for this book is available from the British Library.

All experiences and observations in this book did not take place at Hamstead Hall Community Learning Centre unless otherwise stated. The names of all children have not been disclosed due to Child Protection and confidentiality.

RAMP® - Raising Achievement Mentoring Programmes is a registered trademark

This book is available online and all good bookstores.

In Loving memory

This book is in memory of Moyra Josephine Healy, who was more than a teacher to me. Her undeniable passion for people and the fact that she loved every child that she came into contact with has made an unforgettable impression on my life. "If you love someone, you will let them go" is a statement that she shared with me and a class full of students at the age of 14 which has stayed with me ever since.

Moyra, thank you for showing me such kindness, and what the power of having a caring teacher can be. May you rest in peace.

January 28th 1951 - January 11th 2012

Testimonials

"I was captivated by Herman from the first time I heard him speak about his vision of helping children who the education system is failing. This is no pie in the sky social dreaming; Herman's work is based on experience and solid achievement. When he speaks about what's happening to the young people who need help in our education system, you hear a truly authentic account of unnecessary despair and you hear the voice of someone who knows how to make it better.

It's hard to overestimate the importance of this work; if it can be made available more widely it will have an almost unimaginable transformational impact on our society. "

Mike Harris founding CEO of First Direct bank and Egg bank plc. CEO of Mercury Communications and Chairman of One to One (later operating as T-Mobile).

Herman talks about his life, about his work and about education with a real passion. His commitment to young people and their aspirations is almost tangible; he believes in young peoples' right to aspire to be more than they are, and what's more, has been there himself. Herman's story is inspiring and empowering and I wish him luck with the next part of his journey.

Eileen Hinds - Independent Education Consultant

Herman's story goes to show the rewards we all can reap when we dedicate passion, focus and time to finding out what it is we are called to do. His hard graft, the ways he consistently learns from his varied careers, many potential setbacks and his persistence to fulfill his own full potential through championing every child's right to have a mentor is inspirational.

In fact his vision for every child having a mentor has the potential to create the revolution within the education system young people, parents and teachers need today.

So Herman's book is a refreshing, honest and human story of how one man's own journey to find the treasure inside became the beacon of possibility and empowerment for young people, their families and our wider society.

My question is once you have read Herman's book - what steps can you and will you take to make 'Every Child having a mentor' a reality?

Anna Sexton, Community developer & activist, accredited Coach and mentor

Dedication

I humbly dedicate this book to my wife Donna Marie Stewart who has been such a support to me during the time of me writing this book. Donna, you are my best friend, my soul mate, a trusted confidant and a mentor to me. Whilst writing this book, I was faced with many ups and downs and during these times you have always supported, comforted and encouraged me. Baby, for this reason, I dedicate this book to you and I thank you for your love, patience, understanding, kind words and actions which I am deeply grateful for. We did it x 143

Acknowledgements

Success is rarely achieved by a solo effort, and for this reason, I would like to show my appreciation to the following people who have supported me on my mentoring journey and the writing of this book.

I would like to say thank you to my mother, Claudette Cameron-Ferguson who has been a great mentor to me and to my Father Fitzroy Stewart for doing what he could. I would like to thank my sister Kedar for making me aware of mentoring as a career. I would like to thank my daughters Saffron, Serae and Emrah Stewart for being so patient with me and how busy I have been. Thank you very much for being a motivation and blessing to me. Thank you Kendrick Morris, Kate Emson, David Brown, Sukhbir Farah, Dennis Edwards, Dorret Jacobs, Sandra Sterling, Manjit Uppal, Adrian Mccollin, Carolyn O'Sullivan, Vivian Hoyte, Scott Jordan & Kevin Tubbs and all the other staff at Hamstead Hall Community Learning Centre for such a wonderful experience of friendship and a dynamic place to learn my craft. I would like to say thank you Brian Wardle, Jane Spilsbury and Hayley Donough for their support during my work for the city. I would like to thank Antony Brown for all his support, Constance aka Connie and all the KPI's who have helped me progress during this journey. I would like to thank Joanne Benjamin - Lewis for all your editing work for the book - you have really helped with your insight and sensitivity of how to communicate my message. I would also like to show gratitude for all the work done by Anna Sexton, Jan McKenley, Dr Kim Jobst, Andrew Saunders, James Richards, Marcellus Lindsay, Leesa Daymond & Eileen Hinds. I thank you all for reviewing, proof reading, your words of wisdom and timely contributions for the book. I would also like to thank Mindy Gibbins-Klein for her support, belief and patience during this project, Emma Herbert and those at Ecademy Press, Marianne Hartley for her valuable work on the cover, Ingrid Marn for the beautiful photography and Neil Coe for the great attention to detail on the inlay design. You have all done a wonderful job.

I would like to say thank you to Karl George MBE for all the support and mentoring that you have given me, Michael Ekwulugo, Carlton Jones, Mike Harris, Denzil Edmeade, Martin Oguzie, Akil Gordon-Beckford, Steve Richards, Richard Daley, Curtis Norville, Alison-Gove Humphries, Judy Simpson for all you have done to help me on my mentoring journey and making this book a reality. Finally, I would like to thank my Lord Jesus for being my rock and carrying me along this journey.

Foreword

"Every Child Needs a Mentor" is more than an insightful and compelling treatise on the overwhelming need for intervention to save a generation. This book brings an insight into the life of a young Black male and the factors that took him from the dangers of the inner city streets of Handsworth to sports; from sports to the stage; and from the stage to the schools on the very streets that could have consumed him.

Herman Stewart is a man of principle and integrity – with a talent for inspiring people. My first experience meeting him was during my days as a co-host of a radio show. He was instantly recognised by those in the studio as a man of outstanding talent with the ability to weave words into a tapestry of mental images and compelling emotion.

Herman uses his 'way with words' in this, his first book, to make a clear statement of what mentoring is and what mentoring is not. Importantly, he does this in a way that will ignite your own desire to step out of the shadows of uncertainty and into the light of action to play a part in the lives of our children and future leaders of our country.

I have seen him grow and earn the right to be called "Mentor of Mentors". I witnessed the turning point in his music career when he chose the narrow path of integrity over the lure of fame and further success in a genre that no longer inspired him. This book tells the story of how and why.

From Herman's humble beginnings and the tough decisions that he took in his early years all the way to the development and delivery of his revolutionary approach to making mentoring accessible to a generation that is crying out for help.

His story takes us back to some of our own key decisions and helps us to realise that we have all been mentored or have mentored to some degree. This book will open your mind to your own potential as well as the life - and world - changing benefits that can be realised when each child is given a helping hand through a good mentor.

Herman is a role model in so many ways and is, to me, a reminder of the power of passion and purpose.

"Every Child Needs a Mentor "is a reflection of Herman, the man, the father, the friend and the mentor. He has taken his experiences and his talent to help others to achieve more and sheds light on the present state and possible future for mentoring in the UK.

This book is more than a story of the life of the man that I call a friend; it is a call to children, parents, teachers, governors, the business community and the government of the land. The message is clear and simple. "EVERY Child Needs a Mentor"

Marcellus Lindsay

Contents

Introduction...

The title "Every child needs a Mentor" has managed to raise a few eyebrows and evoked a few comments along the way. Some may feel every child does not need a mentor, but I would simply ask why not? The real issue is not whether every child needs a mentor but, what is your perception of mentoring? As that may be more of an issue.

Who would you say needs mentoring, a child who is not doing particularly well and has a few emotional imbalances which can result in bad behaviour? Or is mentoring for a child who is well behaved, has great ability and is clear where they are going in life? You may believe only one of the above needs mentoring but, I can assure you that both would need mentoring for different reasons, even though in main stream education those who are considered to be "alright" are unlikely to experience being mentored. However, I do not agree with this train of thought and the common practise that ignores the needs of the majority of children in our schools in the UK, as we are on the verge of losing a generation.

I believe every child has a seed of greatness within them and potential that needs mentoring support to come to fruition. For this reason, I believe every child needs a mentor. For years I have observed that those who receive quality mentoring have an advantage over those who don't, as they experience the benefits, knowledge, skills, contacts and insights of their mentor whilst the others have to work out everything for themselves. During this process the mentee is exposed to gems that you would not learn on an academic course or within a classroom setting but, only by the lessons of life and experience. These lessons that are applied can accelerate the mentee's growth, progress, confidence, insight and success in less time. Simply because the mentor's hindsight becomes the mentee's foresight! And this is why we need to mentor our younger generation.

Some of the best examples to illustrate my point could be found in the following mentoring relationships: David Beckham was mentored by Sir Bobby Charlton, Sir Richard Branson was mentored by Sir Freddie Laker and Eminem was mentored by Dr Dre. Whether it is real life or fiction we see mentoring play a key part, even in movies such as the Matrix where Neo was mentored by Morpheus and in Star Wars we see Luke Skywalker being mentored by the mysterious character Yoda. Even in reality programmes such as the X Factor we see the potential stars being mentored by your Gary Barlow's and Kelly Rowland's who have done it before, so their experiences fast track the contestants. We can even go back as far as Aristotle mentoring Alexander the Great or even further back with Moses mentoring Joshua in Bible times. So it is a known fact that mentoring is tried and tested and has worked across centuries, industries, cultures & disciplines and needs to be used more with our young people who are in desperate need of our support and not our judgment.

So my question is… why is mentoring not viewed more positively in main stream education? In every other field whether it be business, sports or media mentoring is viewed as something highly desirable and to be sought after. However in education, mentoring has so many negative connotations and is seldom accessed by those who truly desire it, or those who urgently need mentoring receive it too late. I have witnessed this too many times and to me this is wrong and is one of the reasons why there are so many disconnected young people in our schools, homes, communities, prisons and universities. I am passionate about changing that and this is the reason why I have written this book.

I believe every child deserves a mentor and that it is their birth right to experience their potential, and if their parents or family members are not able to help them all the way then we should. It is not a nice thought to believe that many children are dying on the inside because they are not being helped to discover or experience their passion for life as their buried potential lies dormant within them. For this reason, my dream is to facilitate mentoring experiences for every student within education. I know this is a big challenge and I do not even know how I will get there, and I may or may not achieve it, but no one should doubt my commitment to do all that I can to make it happen. And regardless of me getting there or not, something great will be achieved on the way.

I am not naïve of the challenges that such a vision will present but I aware that this is something that I could not do by myself. So I am looking for partners and allies who also have a passion for young people and would like to see this vision happen. And when I say every child needs a mentor, I truly mean mentor in the broadest sense as every parent, older sibling, relative, teacher, youth worker and those who are faith, business and community leaders are all mentors and will all be needed to play a crucial part to support our youth.

About the book itself: I have literally poured everything I am into these pages which makes it more than a book to me. I share my journey, the ups and downs and the challenges and victories I have experienced along my way. Inside you will find case studies from mentees and parents who share their views on mentoring. Included there are also quotes from mentees from mentoring sessions. As a bonus; for those who are mentors, coordinators or are just considering to develop a mentoring programme, I have included insights and strategies to help you on your journey. Finally… for those who would like to try the mentoring experience, I have included a few reflective activities for your benefit.

So I thank you for your time as it does mean a lot to me. And my hope is that my burning desire to see every child receive a life line through mentoring consumes your heart as it does mine.

Herman Stewart

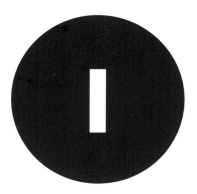

Humble Beginnings

The Impetus

I stood at a crossroads in my life, but this one was different. Up to this point, I have had many crossroads where I had to make very difficult decisions but, I could sense that everything depended on the choice I was about to make. I had now arrived at a place in my life and on the verge of making a decision that would dramatically change the direction of my life, which was quite scary. I was outside my comfort zone as I experienced fruitlessness and being barren which had become my new norm but, deep down I knew I was worth more. My life was about to be turned upside down, I was afraid but had no other options.

What was there to lose?

At this juncture, I was a recognised professional recording artist who was considered to be a best kept secret. In the urban music industry, I had peers and journalists who were citing it was my time and that I was the next big thing. After featuring on a number of releases, my debut album titled "The Sealer" was eagerly awaited by journalists, radio DJs and doting fans up and down the country. Things looked like they couldn't get any better but, even though all of the above was true, my time was running out! At the age of 25 the game had now changed for me, as I had just become a father and had another mouth to feed.

"My time was running out!"

Anyone who knows the music game, which is one of the most competitive and cut throat industries you can be in, knows you can have the fame, the fans, feature in the magazines, be on the radio and various music channels and still be on Job Seekers Allowance (JSA) and signing on! This was weird to me, as I was on MTV but I was still going to the job centre and hoping that I never encountered the most difficult employment officer who would interrogate me about my job seeking exploits! I was not reluctant to work because I was previously working temporarily in offices doing business administration for years, but I was also working at establishing myself as a professional recording artist which was a full time gig. Previously, I was told to make sure I had a plan B, to which I would reply "my plan B is plan A!" because I considered I had a job (being an artist) that would one day pay off, and I was experiencing all the fruits of success but, still I had not cracked it! "How do I monetise fame, respect and a strong street kudos into financial security?" This was a lingering question on my mind as I now needed money for baby essentials.

I put the baby essentials first but, what about me? As you cannot give what you do not have. However the brutal truth was, I had been chasing this music dream for nearly a decade and had been so close and so far without achieving any significant monetary success. I had become accustomed to living in my future, floating in my present and waiting for my time to come, which was now taking its toll. I was living a life of sacrifice, due to the dream and staying available for years by not being job bound so I was doing months then years (months accumulated) of temping, office work and business administration. At times, I was doing some of the most soul numbing and mundane jobs known to man, just to keep my dream alive, whilst living a double life as a professional recording artist. I was totally convinced and driven that I was going to make it! I could see it at present, but just couldn't touch it!

"Frustration is frustrating"

How long?

I could tolerate all of the tedious jobs that I had just because of the dream and where I could see myself going... that one highly desired destination... Stardom! But the life of a writer, recording artist, promoter, label owner and marketer was hard as well as taxing. Believe me, the lifestyle I needed to maintain to be a successful song writer and recording artist is not the most conducive to civilian normality. Hours are unsociable; nights are long, writing stints commonly started after 12am and usual ended around 4am. So late nights of writing and recording till the sunrise and sleeping till late afternoons was the norm. Unwittingly, I had become nocturnal (I didn't even notice because it was so normal) and this was accepted willingly or begrudgingly by close ones and family members, even though at times, I could not see or was not selfless enough to care. To reflect on it now, it was quite selfish but, I was blinkered, focused, determined and intense. I will make it! In fact I must make it! My plan B was plan A and my dictionary lacked one word beginning with F – failure, so giving up was not an option.

"To reflect on it now, it was quite selfish"

Where was I?

Back to my crossroads, with an extra mouth to feed this raw paternal instinct kicked in that overrode my self-centred ambitions, to make it as an artist at any cost. I now had responsibility, I had to grow up. I now had a child that was in need of resources which I did not have, as they were all banked in the future: the Aston Martin DB7, the holiday homes around the world and the endless zero's in the bank! But they were not present now. The reality of it was I was going through a mid 20's crisis, living in the inner city of Kings Norton on the outskirts of Birmingham. In fact I was secluded and alone in a flat where no one knew me. I had done this by choice, as I needed a break from the hustle and bustle of Handsworth. I now lived in a place where no-one would dare risk coming so far unannounced! I was without steady income and broke! At times, I was so anxious to turn on the heat even when it was cold because I was already using the emergency backup reserve. I'm not sure how, but this had become my everyday life. But I still had a dream.

"Things really needed to be different"

When I look back, there were times I must have been depressed or I did not want to face the world. The reason being I would just stay in my bed even though the day was passing me by and I was wide awake. And once my flat was broken into, it just intensified my need for drastic change. I felt really scared and I was now going to bed prepared to protect myself against intruders who may return again. Things really needed to be different.

Change had come...

I was invited to move in with my sister, which was a blessing and brought me back into Handsworth - my place of familiarity and comfort, but things were far from comfortable. It was a ride I definitely wanted to come off, but it seemed no-one was cutting me any slack; at least I viewed it that way. I was tired and had enough of being deprived when I knew I deserved better, had greatness within me and more to offer the world, my child and partner. I simply could not accept this circumstance as my lot. You see, even though I went through all of this, I still dreamt of better days and was fully persuaded they would come regardless of how. Better days would come. But they were just taking far too long and my tolerance was wearing out! I was just so tired and needed a rest from myself, my thoughts and my life which was a relentless hamster wheel.

Question: Are you aware of how valuable you are and the greatness that is within you?

Home from home

From time to time, I surrendered to London where my mum was now residing. This was where I went to have a mum to son chat and eat some good old fashioned Caribbean comfort food. The last few times when I went to visit her I was definitely on my last legs as I was exhausted and did not know where to turn. Whilst at my mother's I shared how I was feeling and experiencing life and she could see that it was taking its toll on me (my mum only disclosed the depth of her concerns when I had passed through this phase). While at my mum's, I had a college prospectus as I considered my future whilst at my crossroads. There were a few things that I had firmly decided...

> "This decision was great and got me out of limbo."

1. I no longer wanted to continue with my music career

2. I needed a career that I could enjoy and earn a living from

   And

3. I no longer wanted to do temporary work as I needed consistency.

This decision was great and got me out of limbo but the eternal conundrum was what exactly could I do? I was now 25 years young and I had not done anything else for the last 9 years since I left school in 1991, except football.

Kenny Daglish from Harry Parkes

Football was my first love! When I was at school I never took learning as seriously as I should have, because football was my main interest. At this point, I could have really done with having a mentor. I really enjoyed the social aspects of school i.e. the friendships, community and fun etc., but I just didn't fully grasp the meaning of school, and since I was good at football, I put all my eggs in one basket. I was told by my mother, relatives and teachers the same regurgitated message of "do well at school so you can get a good job" but after a while that just bounced off as I became desensitized. I never listened and was not receptive and that was the problem, I was so determined to become a footballer – I could think of nothing else. This went back to the tender age of 7-8 years old, whilst playing in my garden on the concrete in my first football boots, I was in love. This passion cost my family a couple of windows and one resulted in my precious leather caser ball being stabbed! I can see it now; I cried so much to see my ball lose its life. That was me - a football fanatic.

"I was so determined to become a footballer – I could think of nothing else."

I'm gonna make it!

At the tender age of 10 years old I was scouted as I was playing in a football final (which we won). Once I started St John Wall Secondary School, I was preselected to play for the District which I did through my school life. I believed I never needed academics (so I thought); I just needed to continue playing football. I could have really done with a mentor during this time as my thinking was so limited.

My blinkered attitude was not helped by being selected to play for the Great Britain Catholic Schools under 15's National Football team, as this confirmed that football was the area I would be focussing on. I was playing alongside players like the legendary Paul Scholes of the formidable Manchester United! So this just gave me more fuel to believe I would be a footballer, which made it worse for me. I now had the view that a professional football career was definitely on the cards and in a sense this left me ill prepared for revision, exams and leaving school. So, when I left school and I was not enrolled into another football team straight away, my focus dwindled. Accompanied by injury, a love for clubbing and a lack of discipline, football slowly went down the pan. Even though on a number of occasions I tried to resurrect it, the football just slipped more and more out of my hands.

Question: Is there anything that is slipping out of your hands that you are finding difficult to let go of?

Autodidact

Due to my love of football and how sure I was that I was going to be a professional, I had a nonchalant attitude towards school. I can honestly say I never made the most out of education to my own peril, and whilst in school I would doodle and write lyrics. I am not advocating that this is a good thing but it's what I did and I also practised my signature hundreds of times as I believed that at some point soon, I would need to do autographs. So in the back of my maths book I would write rhymes for fun and never thought much of it because I was focussed on becoming a footballer, until I had repetitive groin injury and this dream was slipping away. I then started to take music seriously.

On this new passion, I would spend hours practising verses to my songs and making noise in my house. I thank my mum for her patience because I did test them! I formed a group called MSI (Microphone Stranglers Incorporated) and later we paired up with a group called Asylum. As a group we went on to open up for some of the biggest artists in the world between 1994 and 1997 such as Busta Rhymes, Wu Tang Clan and Keith Murray. We were the first group from Birmingham to release a Hip Hop album and were on Tim Westwood's Radio One show, Galaxy FM, Numbers "279" Choice FM show and also had a video on MTV. We were well renowned and on our way to great things, but things happened with the group and just like Steve Jobs was fired from the company he made, I was ousted from the group I made! Even though this was so painful and plunged me into a short time of feeling so lost with another passion of mine thwarted, this was for my benefit.

Where did I go from there?

Since I still had the music bug, the separation didn't stop me, so I continued on and made plans to go America and with some help from Dean Alexander and Marcellus Lindsay I had meetings with a variety of record labels in New York such as Def Jam, Island, MCA, Violator & Motown who were interested in my music. A representative from Motown records was interested in me but wanted me to put on a London accent, so I sounded more like what they considered to be English. 'English' Due to the fact I was not prepared to fake my twang, I did not even go back to Motown Records for a second meeting, even though they were awaiting my call. So I came back to England and started up my own record label with my close friend James Richards and I called the label Dappa Dann Entertainments. We released the first material which was a seven track E.P (Extended Play), which was well received by many DJs and was reviewed in various magazines. This was a great start as I was now solo after leaving the group; I was still receiving loads of support from old fans as well as gathering many new ones. I then met Antony Brown aka Frikshun who was a prolific music producer who became a very good friend and part of the team. His music was world class and brought what we were doing to another level. Since the EP was released I had good feedback and we had interest from a larger label that was ready to release the EP in Europe. We then made a Joint Venture deal to record and release more material but things started to slow down. During this time, I had my first daughter and a lack of finance, success, direction, and all of the above brought me to the crossroads where I now stood in the year 2001 at the age of 25. I was also considering Christian faith as I was becoming more aware that I needed more out of life and had to be true to my heart that desired a different way of living. I recognised that there was more to human life than just existing or what I could experience with my 5 senses, which was making me more curious. So from my choices of no more football, no more music and no more temping my dilemma was heightened by the fact I did not know what I wanted to do, plus faith was now on the horizon.

"I know what I want to do, I want to do counselling."

Now back to London... as I contemplated over this college prospectus I was really lost. This was the first time in my life I didn't know what I wanted to do. So I relied on my inner instinct and just skimmed over the different subjects then I spotted "counselling". I was not sure then but it all now makes sense counselling really resonated with me. I said mum, "I know what I want to do, I want to do counselling" and she said something to the effect of "you will be good at whatever you do son". So I had my answer, my direction and my new frontier. I was ready to embark on the pursuit of counselling.

Activity – The Impetus

1. How do you feel about where you are in your life right now? Could you explain below

2. List 3 things that you are personally pursuing in your life and in their order of priority?

3. Is the pursuit of your priorities giving you what you ultimately desire in life?

Note: If possible make some space for yourself when completing these activities so you can reflect without distraction. Create a slot for a self mentoring session so you can get the most out of these moments.

He Who Dares Begins

"Every journey begins with one step" and I was about to take mine on this new journey. It was July 2001 and when I arrived home from London, I planned to visit my local college in Handsworth. For the September 2001 academic year, there was an open day which I attended to research my counselling options. I was interviewed by a nice lady and a man who said I would be good at counselling as the man commented "you have a face for counselling" (I guess it was complimentary). So after the interview, I was told I could join the course in September! I was so happy as my new life was taking shape.

September 2001! New season

As I joined the counselling group this was a very new experience as I was just good old normal me instead of being this recording artist. It felt funny because I was undercover like Eddie Murphy in "Coming to America" as he searched for his new Queen (which I found also). In my other life I was highly popular due to my music and football but I was fed up of the hype and was now satisfied and enjoyed being an unknown student. For this matter, I really wanted to enjoy this time of self development so I made a conscious decision to not make anyone aware of my music persona.

My tutor said the first person you must counsel is yourself! Which I found a bit scary but, I was looking forward to the challenge. During one of my counselling lessons, a fellow student named Michelle shared with me she was attending a mentoring course in the same college and insisted "you should do it, you would be good at it", so I took her advice and asked "when is the next lesson?" And she replied "tomorrow" so I made up my mind there and then that I would attend, there was something in this mentoring thing to explore.

A Pram, A baby and a long run!

So on this bright September morning, I got up on purpose with purpose! I had to drop off my daughter Saffron who was around 18 months old to nursery and I had to get to college to enrol on this mentoring course. I thought, since the course had already started to avoid embarrassment, I wanted to get to college early so I could speak to the lecturer before the class started. I had to get my daughter and myself ready, got her pram, strapped her in and off we went! I was on a mission and was doing some power walking like those professional walkers in athletics! The journey was around 2.5 miles and it was going to be tight to get to the college on time. By the time I arrived at the Nursery, I realised I only had around 15 minutes to get to college and that was around another 3 miles walk! I then started to run... I didn't have any bus fare and never had time to wait for the bus anyway. I was running and talking to myself and telling myself not to stop, come on Herman you have got to make it! It was like my life depended on me getting to this college and early! So I could see the lecturer before the lesson as planned. I was running and panting and stopping and jogging and walking and running and holding my side (as I started to get a stitch) it was painful but it needed to be done. As I reflect back, this was some serious pursuit of happiness type of stuff!

As I got to the college, I got there just in time as the class started and I asked to speak to the tutor outside the class. I must have looked a sight as I panted and grasped for air but I did not care! When I was composed enough, I asked if I could join the class and with a smile Ms Jenny Brown, as if she was admiring my efforts to get to college she said "yes". As I was told to sit down and join the class I sensed a victory and the ushering in of something new into my life which was beyond my wildest dreams as I look in hindsight, I could not imagine the positive implications of me being seated in that class but,

I just could not stop sweating! I was sweating and I had no tissues. It was embarrassing but the victory of being in the class was a comforting distraction.

Football again...

Old habits die hard and some things you just can't shake. I don't know how, but I was roped into playing football again. My friend Richard Daley was the manager of a local football team called "Handsworth United" and he convinced me that it would be good for me to join. Richard knew how to push the right buttons as he was passionate about football like me, so I thought ok, why not. Life is so funny because this time football was going to lead me to my true calling.

On this Saturday, we were playing away so we had to meet up and drive in cars, so we gathered up to make the journey. Many arrived on time with some being fashionably late and turning up like superstars with swagger. It was ironic because I was already in Justin's (the assistant manager) car but, I was compelled to leave and go into Steve Richard's car who was my team mate. I was not to know but, this intuitive switching of vehicles was about to change the direction of my life.

 Question: Have you done anything recently to change your Life into how you would like it to be? And if not, is there a reason for your delayed action?

We were now ready to go; there was me, Steven and his daughter who was with us. During the drive Steven who I called "Stevie" started a conversation that went something like this:

Stevie: "So H, what you up to?"

Me: "I am at college studying at present"

Stevie: "So what you studying bro?"

Me: "Counselling and mentoring"

Stevie: "Mentoring? Yes H, that's good. We need more young black men like you doing this work as the young boys need it!"

"We lost, but in hindsight I had actually won."

I then enquired about what Stevie was doing and he shared he was a youth worker and was working with some challenging young people in a children's home. Stevie then shared "I am working with some boys from Hamstead Hall with Judy Simpson (the ex-Great British Athlete and ex-Gladiator Nightshade), who could do with some help from someone like you". He then asked if he could speak to her and give her my number which I said was fine. So we arrived at the away ground and played the match. We lost, but in hindsight I had actually won. We then drove back home reasoning about many things as we looked forward to some good old traditional Saturday soup as a remedy to our injuries and a night's viewing of Match of the Day.

One thing leads to another...

A few days later, I received a phone call from Judy Simpson. As we spoke on the phone she made me aware of the work she was doing with the boys and what I could possibly do to help. On the conclusion of the phone call, Judy invited me to the school on Friday to meet the boys, which I accepted. Not really knowing what to expect, on Friday I visited the school and as I crossed the threshold of the school gate which I had not done for around a decade, I had a little anxiety, but I was excited as I needed this new opportunity. So I met with Judy who was lovely and she was doing some great work with the young black boys. However, Judy believed that these young boys needed a young man to speak to them who they could respect and ultimately develop a more meaningful relationship with. I could understand where she was coming from and I assured her that I would have a talk with them.

What's anger management?

On my first visit, I was javelined head first into the deep end. I was approached by a Head of Year (HoY) who asked me if I knew anything about anger management, as she had a pupil who was experiencing some real anger issues. However, I had never heard of that term but I got the gist of it so I answered..."yes" so I was then pushed even deeper into the deep end as I now had to deliver some impromptu work. The HoY asked me to have a session with this boy immediately, which was quite intimidating as I never knew the boy or fully understood what his need was, but now I was going to have a mentoring session with him. So I sat down with this year 11 student who was quite big in figure, to facilitate an anger management session. And not having all the details I really had to think on my feet. So as I started to speak to this student I found him to be fine. He was warm, calm, humorous, perceptive and articulate about himself and his feelings. I was bewildered. The reason being, I never experienced, heard or seen any reasons for why this student needed an anger management session. So we hit it off straight away and he was glad to meet with me and wanted to see me again, so I had my first mentee and mentoring session. This was a good experience.

Someone pass me the floats!

My second mentee was not as easy and was by no means straight forward. This pupil was around 6′2 and was definitely attending a local gym! He could easily push more weights than I could and I had around 10 years on him. He was seen as a threat to be in school due to an incident that had occurred previously and for this reason he was not allowed to attend school full time and was placed on a part time – time table. This may have been better for the school but was not necessarily better for the student. He was bright and had the ability to achieve good grades hence the school still working with him. However, this pupil had some real issues which were very challenging and draining to deal with. This was a real test to see if mentoring was for me or not, at least it would show if I had what it took to be a mentor.

"I could understand his frustrations and doubts."

"I can't do it!"

The first major task I had was to convince him that he "could" do well and achieve the grades he needed, regardless of his circumstance. This was a real challenge because he was persistently adamant that he could not do it! My first level of work was simply to get him to say that he was able. Session after session he would defy my enthusiasm and optimism about his future which he just did not accept and, even worse, he could not see. But, this was now a mission because if he could not say he could, then we were off to a non starter. We did a variety of things i.e. we met in school, we met outside of school, we ate and spent time together and over a few sessions he was gently warming to my infectious enthusiasm for both of our futures and that he could do it. But the amount of time that he had spent outside of school due to becoming a part time student and the amount of time he had left was making it very difficult for him to achieve his goals, so I could understand his frustrations and doubts.

Confrontation

There was a time in the office when we were having our one to one session and we were having one of our "you can do it" and "I can't do it" bouts but this time it was different. I am not sure why or what had happened this time but even though I was challenging his pessimistic disposition this time he was really getting mad and was being antagonistic as though I was against him. For this reason, I had to man up and be very assertive to challenge him which was a risk as he could probably pick me up, literally! And his anger was going in that direction! But as he peaked, he just broke down crying and sobbed as he shared he just didn't feel that he could do it with the time he had left and I felt for him. He also expressed that he was under so much pressure to achieve academically as well as the other issues he was facing at home. He never lived with his father as he lived abroad and he was not seeing eye to eye with his Nan, who he was living with. So he had a lot on his plate for a 15 year old. I just empathised with him and encouraged that he kept focused and that we could do it together. I urged him to do the work set by the tutor, as the school was giving him additional tutorial and extra lessons but he still could not access some vital lessons. With the issues at home, I shared with him concerning the complexities of life at times and made him aware he would overcome them. I shared with him some of my challenges that ultimately made me stronger and it was making him stronger also.

Believing is seeing

We plugged and plugged on and he did what he needed to do with the additional support from a small net of staff, Audrey and Miss Emson who also believed in him. Miss Emson is one of the most pastorally hearted members of staff you would ever meet. She has a true compassion for children and an endearing nature but if ever the children got on her bad side it was trouble as she can shake the walls of a corridor by the power of her voice raised. Miss Emson who is known to me as Kate also became my line manager and she wielded great influence which she used to help and benefit the children. With Miss Emson's help and her passion for children, she ensured he got as much help as possible. And guess what - he made it! He got all his work in and did what he needed to do! He not only made it but, he did it in style by achieving 7 GCSEs C and above! Even on a part time timetable with the odds against him.

"He not only made it but, he did it in style by achieving 7 GCSEs C and above!"

On the day of the year 11 prom, I remember seeing him cry whilst being amongst his friends, which was so touching. Here was a young man in a grown man's body that just needed to be understood and supported. He made me proud, really proud and I am even feeling choked up as I am reminded about him and his story. From working with these two mentees, I was quite perplexed at how much these boys were misunderstood by some and how they were wrongly communicating their frustrations too. This seemed to be a regular occurrence concerning children of African Caribbean heritage whose cultural communication was perceived rightly or wrongly. I have also come to find that in some school circles it is too easy to wrongly diagnose and assume a child's issues are an anger management or behavioural matter when their issues can simply be more appropriately based on emotional instability. This is commonly manifested via anger and behaviour which masks a totally different issue as the deeper roots of their emotions need to be addressed, not just the manifestation of the issues. It is easy to identify the symptoms as they are right there in your face, however we must always remember behaviour is usually a "result" of something and so is anger! Whether it is feelings of frustration, anxiety, fear, experiencing injustice or home problems etc. Many of these boys were not understood and this is happening in lots of schools on a national level. So my work was now taking up the form of being an intermediary and an advocate because someone needed to be an interpreter for both sides and bridge the gap that has been forever growing.

Change was here....

To my satisfaction, life was changing so much! I was experiencing true fulfilment, I was seeing lives turn around and to hear young people express comments such as "If you were around earlier I would have behaved and done better from long time" was uplifting. I understood where they were coming from even though some of their behaviour was unacceptable and beyond justification, in these circumstances I would challenge the problem appropriately but, reaffirm their value. I was building up such an affinity with these students and I would always make them aware that I was proud of them and I acknowledged that they had taken steps to becoming better people, but still had room for improvement. I believe one of the most important factors was that I recognised the students were separate from their behaviour. At times their behaviour was naughty but they were not naughty! To draw such a distinction is crucial, because a lack of such distinction is the reason for many young people becoming stigmatised through wrongly being labelled.

Case Study:
Mentee Story Renaldo King
Mentor Herman Stewart

I grew up in an educated family: my mother was a hard working and educated and so was my father, so from birth I was instilled with intellect and potential to achieve. My parents split when I was 8 years old so not only did I have to mature quickly to become the man of the house, I was also confused why this had happened, which caused me to react in a certain way. As well as this, there was no longer a man in the house for me to answer to, or for me to be afraid of getting in trouble. I grew up in a area which can be considered as being a 'ghetto' or just outside the 'ghetto', so from a young age I was surrounded by a lot of negative attributes which you witness in the outside world, and all these aspects combining was developing the person I was to become and my insight on the world, what I felt you had to do or who you had to be to survive and be well known {because as a young person this is what every young person wants}.

Once I left junior school my parents decided to send me to a private school to give me the best opportunity in life, but due to where I was living and the things I had already experienced in life I was bringing that mentality to this school, and eventually after the 1st year I was excluded for a fight that initially wasn't my fault. At the time I never cared, I just wanted to go to school with all my junior school friends and friends from around my area. I was already popular around the area due to playing football and the friends I had and I wanted to lavish that lifestyle. Year 8 {big sigh of relief and excitement} I started Hamstead Hall, and it felt like home all my friends were there. I had all the attention from the girls. I was the man. For the first couple years, my behaviour was mild. The teachers tolerated it but by the time I got to year 10 there was a dramatic change. I was heavily involved in the street life so my mentality was no one can speak to me no one can relate to me, "I'm the man of the house so I don't have to listen to no one". On top of that I developed anger problems which were extremely explosive and at times would scare the teachers and other pupils. It got to the stage where I was suspended so many times and the teachers wanted me gone. The only reason why a particular teacher {Ms Emson} gave my stay consideration was because they could see I had natural intellect and potential as I just got A* in GCSE music a year early, which none of the higher year achieved. The school then gave me one last opportunity - they brought in someone to be my mentor/anger management. When I was first told I was going to have a mentor/anger management tutor I laughed. I thought no one can change me, I'm not going to tell him anything, I'm basically going to bully him like I was doing to everyone else. The only positive thing I got out of it was being able to exercise my power and popularity by telling all my peers the extent the school is going to to try and correct my bad behaviour.

It was time to go to my first session. I didn't know what to expect I just expected it to be a doss - an easy way to get out of the lessons I hated. Then I walked into the room and saw a young person, not an old man, someone dressed just how I would dress, someone who spoke just like me and someone who seemed they genuinely wanted to help me. As we began to speak I started to realise he understood where I was coming from as he had already experienced what I've been through in my life, had experienced things I hadn't been through but were yet to come and related to my perspective as a young person while trying to help me to develop my character and view in life.

As the sessions went on throughout the weeks I started to open up more and reveal more of my life to the mentor, comfortable that this information wasn't going anywhere apart from between me and him, he respected me and I now respected him which contributed to my school work getting done, my anger calming down - even if I was to get in an outrage, the teachers just called him - and the respect he had for me not to embarrass me in front of the teachers but to guide me away was for my best interest. I would listen to him which diffused a lot of situations. It also helped having someone there who wasn't against you, who was like your solicitor in court only if you were in the wrong you were in the wrong, he wouldn't try prove you right but he would see why the situation happened and how to get the best positive outcome, and if you were right he would fight till the end. My mentor not once tried to act as a teacher or was seen as a teacher, which is why for someone to deal with a child like me they had to be like me while being a role model at the same time. He always remained himself but when it was time to work or do something serious he would get serious and this is what I needed. I enjoyed being with someone who could relate with me on all levels and also a level which I had not yet experienced due to my age. The mentoring never just stopped after his sessions, it was continuous and he was always checking up on what I was doing, how I was doing and if all relevant work was completed while also showing great interest in my personal requirements, which at that time was music {rapping}. All aspects of my life I could go to my mentor, no matter what it was, from the streets to education to music and he would always have a positive answer or how to conduct the situation positively and this is what I needed.

Without having a mentor I feel I would have been kicked out of school. I wouldn't have been understood by the school and would have been seen as just another statistic. The mentor filled the gap between school and pupil and I feel every school and every underachieving young person should have a mentor to give them the chance that I had.

I am now currently a mentor myself in the same shoes my mentor was 10 years ago and because I approach it just like him: dress like the youth, talk like the youth and have been there just like the youth are, now they relate to me like I once did with my mentor and I now have the opportunity to give youth that were once in my situation the opportunity to get to where I am now. I feel once you've been there, you're more passionate, and it's more emotional because you understand the struggle, you understand what it feels like to feel on your own but then you understand what it feels like to get out of it. When you're talking to the young people, teachers with 30 odd kids in the class can't deal with each individually but instead of kicking the young person out of school giving them no hope at all fill the gap, give that child a mentor and a chance for a better future.

"It is so important never to give up! As you never know what is around the corner and how fast your life can change."

My life was turning around

I was also experiencing an internal metamorphism due to my own personal epiphany. I was aware of my personal needs for inner fulfilment as well as my short comings. For this reason, I started to explore faith, its meaning to me and where it was even relevant. This exploration was a catalyst for me as it opened other dimensions to my life and led me to become a Christian which has been very fruitful. I also met the love of my life, my soul mate Donna while we were both studying counselling at college, who is now my beloved wife and the mother of our two girls Serae & Emrah. So my life was now really becoming unrecognisable from what it previously was.

In three's

They say things happen in three's, which was proving to be true in this case. I was now studying counselling and mentoring, found the woman of my life and later became a Christian. I was also being offered a few jobs as a mentor and in the school again! It is so funny how life can quickly change, that's why it is so important never to give up! As you never know what is around the corner and how fast your life can change. So keep holding on and proceed forward as your next step could change everything! I share this with children who feel there is no point or hope because of the challenges of life but there is always hope, there's always a way out, it's just do we believe?

Who dares begins - Activity

1. What 3 things would you like to begin doing in your life now, if possible?

2. Are there any reasons why you have not started any of the three things as of yet? If so could you list them.

3. What do you need in place to start any of the three things you have listed?

4. What things have you started that you would like to complete?

Boundaries, Boundaries, Boundaries

After the success with the few mentees, the effectiveness of my approach was being recognised by teaching staff, senior leaders and more importantly the Head teacher. For this reason, he offered me a secure position, unlike many mentoring arrangements at that time (mentoring employment was predominantly on a fixed term basis) and I was set on par with other staff with fringe benefits. During one of our initial conversations he gave me the following piece of advice: "Work on building positive relationships with teaching staff". I never understood why he needed to say that as it was obvious to do so. But, he was sharing this with me for a reason which I was to find out later in my career and I will speak more on in the book.

As I had been working just with the year 11s who had now completed their GCSEs and had flown the nest and the new year 11s were deemed to be alright (self starters and able), I was now given the new focus of working with the current year 10s. Little did I know that this was to be a baptism of fire! But, everything that I had already learnt in my life was definitely about to come into play as preparation for this phase and would soon to be tried and tested. I definitely had to learn to sink or swim, and fast!

"Work on building positive relationships with teaching staff."

The list

I remember when I was approached by Mrs Humpherson the HoY, who I worked with closely and who was a good mentor to me. For this task she gave me a list of around 15 students who I was not familiar with but they all seemed to have something in common. However, I knew that this list must have contained some characters, because a few teachers who came to know I was working with these students would laugh, shake their heads or simply wished me luck! The truth be known, even though I have become much more refined and adapted well, I came from a very street wise life so young people or people in general who seemed hard to deal with or were considered too far gone were right up my street. I understood that it is all about the 3 R's: Respect, Realness and Responsibility, and if we could work with these 3 R's we would be good.

"It is all about the 3 R's: Respect, Realness and Responsibility."

During this time I found that being a mentor can be a very difficult role to fulfil within a school setting for a number of reasons...

Where do you fit in? Because you may not dress like the traditional member of staff and be in more informal attire, so then you do not naturally slot in with other staff and some teachers may deem you as unprofessional or dressed inappropriately. On the other hand, you could be dressed in a manner that enables you to communicate through clothing that would help you to build rapport quicker and win with the young people because they understand your dress sense as it is very communicative. But, you are also a member of staff so in the grand scheme of things the pupils may also struggle to understand where you fit in as well. For this reason, I have termed being a mentor like being a professional friend to the young person, someone who is friendly but not a friend, due to your professional purpose and context. At the same time you are able to have conversations that they may not consider sharing with someone who they do not have a relationship with.

Let me explain. As an effective mentor you will build a different type of relationship with your mentees that enables you to have a different effect on them. As you influence their understanding and behaviour via building an authentic rapport by befriending them. In turn it can have a profound impact on how seriously they view education, life and school. So the dynamics of the relationships you are supposed to build for the benefit of the school is very different to the one a student may build with a teacher. As the mentee needs to feel they are able to share information with the mentor that is not necessarily school specific and could somewhat be personal, mental or emotional. At the same time by the mentee sharing this information it will impact school as you help them deal with how they balance life and school. This is the reason why I share the term of a professional friend.

In no shape or form as a mentor to children in a school setting, do I believe you should be a friend as this can blur the lines and cause issues. You are a member of staff first and you are also teaching them how to manage a number of relationships with a variety of dynamics also. So it is important that one is careful of not getting too close so that your judgement is not eschewed which will affect the mentor's clarity and ability to be objective when it comes to helping the mentee facilitate solutions. That's why I feel the role has its challenges because it will take great skill and experience to find the balance that helps everyone to benefit. As a mentor you are not a teacher, pupil or peer but you have some attributes of all three which makes the role unique, dynamic and enriching if delivered effectively. But it also takes great skill to manoeuvre in the role within school without being undermined or viewed as a pupil or unprofessional.

This can cause an identity crisis because you can feel like you're in the middle (mediator) on the teachers' side (authoritarian) or on the pupils' side (a traitor or, even worse, unprofessional). The reality of it is... you need to feel alright in your own skin and ready to be perceived wrongly because at times you are not accepted by either side even though you are still instrumental in all parties experiencing the greater good of your labour.

Tricky

What can also make commanding the role tricky is, it is the strength and depth of your relationships that makes you more or less effective. Let me explain... I have been known to retrieve mobile phones that had gone into the school community after going on walkies out of someone's bag or jacket etc. (If I was notified within a reasonable time frame, typically 2 hrs). Now, how I could get that information without the student community feeling like or deeming themselves as snitches (grass). It was because they perceived me to be safe and never looked at me like I was solely a member of staff, even though I never compromised being a member of staff. Now this was highly beneficial to teachers also, because they just wanted the phone back and on some cases even immunity was given. But, how you earned that relationship or gained it could be compromising, because if they saw you as one of them then they would probably do things around you that you're not really supposed to see or even prepared to see for that matter.

There was a time when I was very green and new to the role when I would go and spend time with the students. I was told to do this by my manager who was very senior in the school as she believed it to be effective. As she felt I needed to build relationships with the students and I could also be a deterrent to bad things happening due to me being with them. But, because of the familiarity of the relationship with some of the pupils they treated me like I was one of them, which could put me in an awkward position. For example... if I had seen something untoward and I reported it they would have instantly known it was me as no other member of staff could have known, then the effectiveness of my role within school would be rendered ineffective as they would not trust me. So I had to consciously create boundaries and communicate them to the students, in doing so I learnt how to avoid some of their spots and I made them aware, if I was to venture around and see anything they should not be doing, I would have to share that with senior staff. This was not easy at first as it took a re-shifting of our relationships. So I just kept away like the other staff did even though they may be in the know of some of the shenanigans that could be occurring. But, I did achieve this and we got to the point that when pupils saw me coming there was a lot of fidgeting and even some running which proved I had made that transition, at least partly.

"This was not easy at first as it took a re-shifting of our relationships."

That Hug

I was at the sandwich shop on break duty which usually earned you a free baguette as you managed the queues. As I was just standing there, I was approached by one of my mentees who was a female and before I could do or say anything she just came up to me and gave me a big hug as though I was a friend! This was not only uncomfortable but embarrassing as it happened right in front of some of my work colleagues. I did not know what to do with myself. Even though I knew that the hug from this student was one of friendship as she did this every day to her friends that she respected, both male and female, but, this had never happened to me before and I did not know where to put myself as I blushed profusely.

On reflection, I must take some responsibility for this; it was partly my fault because I must have obviously been so easy-going with the mentees in a bid to get them onside that I did not fashion some very solid boundaries. And in hindsight, I can see the reason for the problem. In my perception, to be a good mentor I had to be able to develop very good relationships with the young people so I would be able to be 'in' with their crowd, in the know and more effective at supporting and challenging them when appropriate. But this position was way too close and is probably like those undercover cop movies where the cop ends up being in too deep! At the same time this must have been slightly perplexing to the students who had to make assumptions or judgements as to how to conduct themselves with me because they knew I was a member of staff and we never communicated outside of school or exchanged numbers or emails or anything like that but being a mentee was also new to them. However, I did not promote or endorse this level of affection that I had received from my mentee, as I was very mindful even though I was very new to the role. I was on a very steep learning curve which was about to get even steeper as I now had to readdress my approach.

Losing to gain

I now had to talk to my mentee concerning what had happened which I was not looking forward to. At the same time it was something that had to be done and could not be avoided. I soon met with this girl and quickly during our conversation I had to bring up what had happened from my perspective and made her aware that it was not appropriate. I expressed that it should not happen again, which she did take a bit of offense to because to her it was innocent and not how it could have been potentially perceived. But she dealt with it graciously.

As she explained herself that she was just treating me like that because I was 'safe', which I totally knew and understood that it was meant to be platonic in nature. But, it was serious to me because obviously it could be misconstrued by others and staff would not take kindly to such gestures between students and staff, which I agree. After the conversation we were both alright at the end of it and moved on. Ultimately our mentoring relationship never recovered and over time deteriorated even though there were no ill feelings. We were not the same anymore and the way we related to each other was mechanical and was not as it was before. But the other worry I now had was the perception of some of the staff who I was trying to win over with my "professionalism" who had witnessed what happened.

"I totally knew and understood that it was meant to be platonic in nature."

You are now one of us, or are you?

I found out quite quickly that being a mentor has its challenges because you have to have a level of informality to connect with the students but, you are also working as a member of staff within an organisation with professional expectations. Due to mentoring not being a traditional role within a school setting and it was so new, many other practitioners didn't really understand it anyway, which never really helped. Because of this, I was always fighting countless battles with the development of the role which at times was seen as intrusive and not complementary to teaching and learning due to its different purpose. Since mentoring was a supportive role and not academic, mentoring was not in the curriculum so any time I had a mentoring session (and I had 15 mentees to see) I would have to borrow someone's curriculum teaching time to see my mentee. This was one of the challenges, but when you had children deemed as naughty some teachers were eager for you to take them out of their lessons! At times the students were sent to me without a request as if I never had anything else to do. Every child needs a mentor but, how mentors are viewed i.e. as a problem fixer etc. This can further pigeon hole your work and turn it into only taking care of children who were in trouble and unwanted by their teachers because of the disruption that they caused in their particular lesson.

Even though this was a truth concerning how some teachers used mentoring and viewed its role and purpose, this was not the case with all teachers. Many teachers were highly supportive and appreciated the work done via mentoring as they could see the bigger picture and also experienced the benefits. Some of my greatest fans were not mentees but teachers who had an understanding of the children and knew that some needed more attention, care and support for them to be able to access learning. They also recognised that they could not offer the level of support needed and were humble enough to admit they were not the best skilled to do so either. So my work was a necessity for the advancement of many students and their teachers "got it" and endorsed mentoring as a much needed support mechanism. However there were some teachers who held dated views that were not connected to this day's reality of the diverse needs that children now present. Some had the view of 'why do you need mentoring?' And "mentoring is for those who are mental" etc. Those teachers were condescending and patronising but also misinformed and out of touch with the generation they now served.

At times I could discern the snootiness of their perceived superior attitudes due to being teachers and me being a mentor. This was confirmed the other day by a highly respected and well distinguished Head teacher (with a knighthood to boot) as we discussed education matters he laughed at some of the attitudes of teachers within his organisation. What he shared was "Us as teachers can be snobs, and some teachers even speak condescendingly of teachers with less qualifications than themselves" he then candidly went on to share an example of how one of his teachers who has a PhD would berate one of their peers with a masters degree!

Anyway, I was aware as a young black man within a predominantly white staffed organisation who was able to earn the respect and cooperation of the students when this was an immense struggle for some staff members could create its own barriers, which I had to learn to navigate. I would not say race has ever been a big issue to me or has it ever been made to be in any organisation I have worked in. However, I am aware of perceptions, stereotypes and prejudices as they do exist even in today's society as we have witnessed in the football world with Suarez and Evra as well as John Terry and Anton Ferdinand. I have also witnessed the sad facts of punitive discrepancies played out to the detriment of some of my mentees. I am not naive and am aware of institutionalised racism just as many are.

I need to strike this balance

You see one of the biggest challenges mentors have whilst striving to be respected by peers, mentees and even parents is... balance. I found my mistake at the start of my mentoring adventure was playing too right field where I was more closely acquainted to the pupils within the learning community which in a sense hindered my ability to be respected as a peer; I would go as far as saying even taken seriously as a professional. But then if I were too close to the staff, hanging out in the staff room drinking tea, and colluding with my colleagues I could have been seen solely as one of them and that would have affected my ability to build trusting relationships with the mentees...

so therein lies a problem! And there is a flip side to being too close with the pupils as they may respect you as a person but not as a member of staff. This creates other problems because it limits how you can deal with the pupils when you need to assert discipline for their learning and betterment. I would experience this when challenging a student who was at the tuck machine in between lessons and when I would tell them to get to their lessons some would still put the money in the machine, look at me, laugh and then run off, knowing who I was, which was highly disrespectful. This tight rope was so hard to walk and incredibly difficult to stay on and after a few goes, I could see how things had to change... but not before one more incident.

"This tight rope was so hard to walk and incredibly difficult to stay on."

I could have lost my job today!

It was the end of the summer term and the 6 weeks' holiday was approaching. The year 10s were going on a reward trip to play some bowling due to being good throughout the year. Since I worked closely with them I was asked to be a part of the staffing team which was always one of the benefits of not being on a structured rota. So we went on the coach to go on this trip and instead of being like a "conventional" member of staff who sat at the front with their peers, I decided to get in with the pupils and sat in the mix at the back. On the way there it was fine, I even had a good one to one with one of my mentees. As we played bowling the boys showed that they had other skills and you could see who was very familiar, with bowling shoes, balls and wooden lanes. However, when we were coming back it was not the same.

As we journeyed back to the school I sat at the rear of the coach. On the journey, someone felt that it would be good to have a friendly prank but, with me being the butt end of the joke. As I sat there someone tapped me on my head and when I looked around everyone's face was straight as a margin. Then I turned around and shortly after the same thing happened again. This time I was like "come on now stop messing about" and then turned around slightly annoyed and hoping that it would stop. This happened again for the 3rd time and I was getting quite annoyed by this time because every time I turned around I did not have a clue who was doing it! Plus they were all laughing at this time because they all knew who it was whilst, I never had the foggiest. I was sitting there and I was trying to think how could I catch the person doing it and if I could turn around with ninja speed to catch them in act but, once again it happened, then I lost it! Oh my life! I got mad with everyone and warned them not to touch me and they knew I was not joking. I was brought down to their level because I was totally sucked in, hook line and sinker and displaying the kind of behaviour I would tell them not to display. I felt so vulnerable and upset; I was truly disappointed that I fell for it. But, I was even more upset about the fact that I was so close to crossing the professional line which would not have been good, plus the end of my work in education, with a crispy P45 on its way. I always strived to exercise restraint with adults in general, so the fact I was a few inches away from losing it with students at work which would have resulted in a dismissal was even more concerning to me.

Six weeks holiday - come on!

That journey could not finish quick enough; I so wanted to come off that coach. For the first time I could not wait to break up from school. I felt that everything had come to a head and I needed to break away. I wanted to go on the six week holiday because I needed the time to create a space in between our familiarity, so that I could have that distance so I could create a new professional stance. This really had to change, as it was it was no longer working for me.

Boundaries, Boundaries, Boundaries - Activity

Whether it is in personal or professional relationships boundaries are essential and I have found them to be imperative in the mentoring relationship. If you find the balance of being informal but formal and a member of staff but personable you will find mentoring a joy. But if you don't find this balance you will suffer. Use this activity to reflect on how you find developing boundaries in your personal or professional life.

1. Are there any boundaries that you are finding a challenge to establish? If so, why?

2. How do you find experiencing confrontation with those who you need to create boundaries with?

3. At worst would you be willing to lose a relationship as a result of establishing a healthy boundary?

4. In the future what could you do differently to insure you set more healthy and productive personal and professional boundaries?

Reinvention

One creature that never ceases to amaze me is the caterpillar. There is no other creature that I am aware of that is so fascinating! Because as a part of its growth and development it totally changes its identity and function! This creature is born of larvae then starts off its life as a caterpillar and then crawls around eating foliage until it is ready. It is then incubated within a cocoon and after its transformational sleep; it comes out no longer a caterpillar but as a butterfly! How remarkable is that? The caterpillar experiences a change of form, colour, function and purpose as it no longer crawls but flies! This has always amazed me and this is what good mentors can help facilitate within a young person's life - stimulate their growth and development.

"The struggle is what gives its wings the strength to fly!"

I share this with young people and make them aware that they have the potential to become more than what they are and they can become that if they do their part! The other thing I find quite intriguing is this transformation is not easy and comes along with its challenges. In the process of the butterfly exiting the cocoon (the place of change) it has a mighty struggle to experience its full metamorphosis. However, without this struggle it cannot fly! So if you ever come across a butterfly exiting its cocoon and you see it struggling never help it out, as the struggle is what gives its wings the strength to fly! So without the initial challenge there would be no flying and they would be resigned to crawling like a caterpillar, which is a bit like many of us!

We were created to experience greatness and soar beyond our limits but, many of us accept mediocrity and find it more comfortable to crawl.

The reality of it was that I now needed my own butterfly experience! I needed to enter my cocoon which was the six week holiday, change and come back like a new creature. And it couldn't come any faster! But to tell the truth this life lesson could not come at a more pertinent time because the summer holiday in school terms is a cocoon in itself.

"My Caterpillar turn Butterfly act and make that transformation!"

A few baritones lower...

During the summer break, many situations changed in the school world. For example, some of boys leave for the holidays with their voices a few octaves higher, return a few centimetres taller with their voices broken and a few baritones lower. Some staff leave for the holidays as spinsters and bachelors to return as newlyweds donning their Mr and Mrs titles with the ring to match. Same for the schools, school positions were heightened or lowered in the School League Table from the consequences of their GCSE results achieved by their previous year 11 students. This would then influence the mood and the tone of the Head teacher's address on staff training day which was usually the first staff day back. For some schools they broke previous records whilst some became present on the then National Challenge register with others just scraping past the 30% 5 A to C GCSE base line to escape the scrutiny of Whitehall. Put it this way, so many things happened in the six week holiday, so for me it was an opportune time to do my Caterpillar turn Butterfly act and make that transformation!

The Mentor's Oxymoron

As a wordsmith, I tirelessly pursued the knowledge of words which fascinate me. I remember when I came across this word "oxymoron". This word means a figure of speech by which it produces a self contradictory effect for example: "bitter sweet", "cruel kindness" or finally "to make haste slowly" etc. Basically the two words don't usually comfortably coexist and I think what I experienced on the coach highlighted the mentor's predicament or the mentor's oxymoron and on that coach I did behave like a moron.

You see mentoring within education is different from mentoring practised in every other industry for a variety of reasons:

1. In education, the mentee is predominantly selected due to a criteria dependant on the schools perception of what mentoring is. So this could be behavioural, pastoral or aspirational. With the latter being less common, pastoral coming in second (the care of students) and behavioural being the most common due to the national deficit model (which I will explain later in the book).

2. In other industries the mentor is head hunted and selected by the mentee and the mentee leads due to their desire to progress within their field i.e. to improve by the help, support, guidance, networks and leverage of their mentor. Last but not least,

3. In sport, business or music mentors usually have a really positive profile and are well sought after as others want to emulate their success. The reason I mentioned this is because in education the mentor's role is to win over the mentee when in other industries the mentee is already won over and desires to win over the mentor to receive their mentorship. For this matter the mentor strives to befriend, build rapport

and have a good relationship with the mentee to enable mentoring to have any chance of success. In this instance the mentor endeavours to be accepted by the mentee to be able to be effective in their profession which at times "can" lead to professional compromise. Now, this will and does cause many issues as there is a fine line to walk concerning this matter which is rarely executed successfully by first time mentors within a school context, because of all the factors that need to be acknowledged and navigated.

One of the compounding factors is: for the mentor to be effective, they must have the ability to build a strong relationship with mentees and preferably their peer groups (as they also influence the mentee). However, sometimes this is to the detriment of developing equally strong relationships with the very teaching staff who are their professional peers. So due to a mentor not being formally dressed and at times lacking a structured approach within the school setting this can affect how they are perceived by their colleagues. I remember being told of a mentor who was a very popular person but, became very isolated and was "kept" outside of the loop by teachers because their relationships were predominantly built with the students. Also if one's personality is needy of "people approval", this issue of building relationships with pupils and the need to be accepted can be compounded. I feel I suffered from a combination of the above at different points of my own mentoring Journey; from the experiences on the coach as well as the hug both these incidents highlighted, the dangers of being "too" close to the students. The fact that I was overly familiar with my mentees had now become a serious issue, which had to be addressed. I needed to establish my boundaries which had not been appropriately set. It was now clear; the students never understood that I was a member of staff and not one of them, which in short spells trouble!

Trading Places

This is one of my favourite films starring Eddie Murphy and Dan Ackroyd. The story was based on two wealthy brothers who made a $1 Dollar bet that they could change the lives of two individuals for better and for worse by changing their lives around. Ultimately, this bet led to the demise of their own personal fortunes and family company. In a nut shell, it speaks of swapping a role and being able to adjust and be successful within your new role. There is much more to it but, that is the long and short of the story and this is what I now needed to do!

I could see some of my challenges ahead because I perceived that I needed to become more like a member of staff than a professional friend or a mentor which was unnerving. One of my advantages of being a mentor was that I was not typically viewed as a member of staff which had its positional advantages as well as having its draw backs. For instance, I found it a challenge to discipline pupils or ask them to take off an offending piece of clothing that they should not be wearing i.e. a cap or head band. So if I was not seen as member of staff, I was released from having to confront students on these matters. I saw this as an advantage however; if I was to ask them the same question some students whom I mentored would not follow the instruction without giving a lot of lip service and banter first. Which I viewed as a disadvantage because the bottom line was I am a member of staff but was not viewed in this way. So I was not looking forward to some of these situations.

Back again, here we go...

Back to the Teacher training day, here we are the first day back after a six week holiday break, staff being reacquainted with each other, exchanging holiday stories, comparing tans and those who were now officially in wedlock were showing off their matrimonial hand wear, over a cup of coffee, which is usually how the school year starts. Our first corporate activity as staff is to be briefed on the August GCSE results, which had improved again. We were in September 2004 and in a few days' time the start was about to embark upon us and I was slightly nervous because I knew things had to be different, but how they were to turn out was not totally in my hands.

In come the kids!

After the teachers were briefed, trained and became acquainted with their new form rooms etc. in came the very children we are paid to serve. I was very aware of my mentees who I had been with on the coach drive (hoping this was forgotten) as they came in with fresh haircuts and the latest jackets. Due to my reluctance to fall into old habits, I was more measured in my approach and even our greetings which were previously very warm and could be deemed as unprofessional were toned down but still friendly. Our rapport was still there and healthy but something had changed especially in me and there was no going back.

What I have come to realise in life is for the new you to come, the old you must go! This does pose a challenge for many hence why some are more willing to reinvent themselves whilst others prefer to stay uncomfortable. One day, I was watching TV with my eldest daughter Saffron who was 11 at the time. We were watching some TV and the adverts were on and our focus was the Barbie doll. My daughter then said something to me which was ironic and rang home the point of change... What she said was "Barbie has been around for years, but Serae and Emrah still like it". What I thought was, this toy manufacturer has had to reinvent Barbie time and time again to keep her relevant and still appealing to the girls of today (she even stars in Toy Story 3) to keep Barbie fresh.

What my point is, we must change but change is not always welcomed or appreciated especially by those who benefit from the old version of you!

What I started to notice as I was changing my approach of how I would engage with these mentees, some of them were now considering me unfair. Some of them would even go as far as saying the swear words which some find offensive and try to avoid "you've changed" which confirmed the changes were taking place and being noticed.

No I haven't!

The challenge of the aspirant mentor is to be able to build meaningful and professional relationships with young people at the same time as being recognised and treated as a credible member of staff. I have noted the word "credible" because, you can be treated as a member of staff but, you are predominantly viewed as a friend of the pupils rather than someone who, if necessary, could also assert discipline concerning young people and were also professional in your approach. I have had experiences with some of my mentees that made me realise deep down they did not respect me, even though they gave me the impression they did. I can remember countless incidents where I would ask pupils not to use the tuck machine and go to their lessons. And some would look in my face, laugh take their money out and still purchase the goods, which I thought was downright cheeky! On some of these occasions, I would confiscate their goods and tell them they could have them back at lunchtime, which was heavily frowned upon but, a necessity to develop our now evolving relationships. I knew I had to get used to being recognised as a changed person because how I was previously, was not the way forward which was proven on the coach trip. And even though this new me was not appreciated as much as before, for me to become who I needed I had to lose the familiarity of some old relationships. In some circumstances, I could confidently say I hadn't changed because my relationships with some students who already had a good understanding and respect for me, we were still alright and the same. But for some mentoring relationships unfortunately, I could not agree more! I had changed because familiarity had bred contempt!

Reinvention - Activity

It is always useful when you become aware when you are going through a transition and it is even more helpful when you can help and roll with the change. You may find this activity useful if you can see the need for change or are going through change but would like to have more clarity during the process.

1. Are there things in your life that are holding you back from experiencing your best?

2. Are there any areas of your life that need reinvention i.e. career, a relationship or a family role?

3. What do you need to do to experience your desired change?

4. Select a person who you could be accountable to and report your progress or challenges on a weekly basis

All things work for the good....

The phrase "All things work for the good" is one of my favourite inspirational quotes and was written by the Apostle Paul and can be found in the book of Romans chapter 8 verse 28 in the Bible. For many who know of Saul who became Paul, he is usually referred to concerning his time on the road to Damascus when He met the Lord and had his own transformational experience. Even if you are not an avid reader of the good book or even a believer of that faith simply take the quote solely on the merit of its eternal optimism, as it is positive thinking at its best! As it believes and hopes that everything "will" ultimately work for the good, even the bad things, for those who love God. This truth has been very reassuring to me and was about to play a significant part in my life, work and successes.

10,000 hours

For anyone who has read the Malcolm Gladwell book "The Outliers" they would have come across the principle of 10,000 hours. This principle stated that for anyone to become world class at any discipline and be cutting edge in their field, they needed at least 10 years of preparation which in a roundabout way equalled 10,000 hours of practise. So concerning where you invest most of your time, resources, and efforts by averaging 10,000 hours you would have a greater opportunity to be better positioned for success than your contemporises who spent less time honing their skill. For me previously, this principle was not encouraging or reassuring at all because where I did invest my 10,000 hours, was not directly linked to the field I was in. But, as I said I was soon to find out that all things "do" work for the good.

That bedroom

In my family home, if walls could talk they would tell stories of untold hours of blood, sweat and tears, nocturnal behaviour and dogged commitment. My undeterred passion border lined on obsession as I wrote and performed rhymes which they now call "bars". Even though in its chosen rustic form of delivery, rapping can be overlooked as art but, in the writing it is all about stanzas, the use of similes, metaphors, adverbs and so on. Thus it is truly poetry and words written from the inner man. Now, in hindsight I believe after a while I became a bit disillusioned and somewhat bitter because I was consistently investing and sowing much more than I was reaping. I could have been labelled a dreamer and unrealistic given the circumstances but I had dreams of living in holiday homes dotted around the world, driving an Aston Martin (champagne coloured DB7 at the time) having enough capital to buy my mother a house and lacking nothing due to being a well accomplished recording artist. I was kind of a rap nerd, with folders and collections of rhymes filed alphabetically in year order. I thought it was great that I was known for my attention to detail and pedantic approach. My fame spread through the community, night clubs, inner cities, prison cells to homes of the United Kingdom and beyond! My music and passion for the art was well known but still I was not earning a decent living for my time spent crafting my passion which was debilitating and painful.

Decisions, decisions, decisions...

One of the hardest things in life I have encountered is to change! Even though it will inevitably come in one way or another be assured, come what may, change will come! But, how do you move from such creature comforts that you have become accustomed to and have become your norm because of the countless years invested to sustain the habit, lifestyle or behaviour. With many sacrifices made, I could justify why I should not give up or change especially with a lingering sense of insecurity while experiencing the "missing bus syndrome", let me explain... have you ever been waiting at the bus stop and there is somewhere you need to get to urgently? And as you are waiting for the bus you are contemplating whether to walk some of the journey (if you're like me) or find another bus service? However, during this time you are experiencing limbo and indecision as you do not want to start walking just in case you get caught in the middle of the 2 bus stops and miss the bus altogether! For those who have experienced this, it can be one of the most unnerving experiences because you really need to get somewhere and you want to travel, but you are conscious that if you travel by foot you would take even longer than if you waited for the bus, what a catch 22! This is exactly how I felt about my music career. I was so close but yet so far, with my 10,000 hours of preparation invested, all the industry specific contacts I had amassed plus the accumulated resources that had been depleted to make this happen to simply walk away was nonsensical! But to me staying and waiting for that bus (the music vehicle) to arrive felt even worse which started to make me feel sick, so I made the decision.... I am going to start walking anyway regardless of whether the bus arrived after my departure, whether it started to rain when I left the shelter, whether it was one of the most foolish decisions I had ever made or it was a masterstroke, I didn't care! Time was ticking and I had to move and only life would tell if I had made the right decision.

Don't you regret it?

Concerning football and my prospects of being a professional "Don't you regret it?" was one of the most common questions I would hear. To deflect it, at times with that kind of macho bravado us men are renowned to display, I would say no (Even though at times, I would privately ponder the same thought!).

I guess I would say a resounding "no" not to be wavered in my new focus of being a recording artist. Undoubtedly, football was my first love, the first thing within my little heart I started to love besides people. I had such a passion for this sport as it gave me a chance to be valued, appreciated and also shine with a recognised ability at a young age. Previously, football was my get out card but, as I grew older and became more distant from the game, I had to come to terms with the reality that my youth was slowly edging behind me and my desire to become a footballer was slipping away, day by day. As I reminisce like the song by Mary J Blige, I remember being a 15 year old teenager hanging out with a friend, sitting on the wall outside their house as we dreamed and compared our prospective careers. We were so competitive as we debated our dreams; my friend was saying she was going to be a recording artist and I was saying I was going to be a footballer and I would drive a SAAB 900! And this was my truth as I could not see anything else, but isn't life funny how things changed and football was now not even on my radar, whilst my old friend did travel the world via the music industry.

"Everything happens for a reason."

Life can be sobering because I have heard untold stories of those who were amazing at football from the community who did not make it either. Hearing scores of stories of bad attitudes, partying the night before matches and turning up to Saturday matches under the influence. Many players who were too big for their boots, who refused to listen to their coaches because they felt that they were God's gift to the "beautiful game". One thing I really recognised in my later years was that talent is not enough! It sounds like a cliché but to me it was a stark reality. I had seen my football talent slip out of my grasp and that of countless others for one reason or another and this was such a waste to me but I have been consistently consoled by the saying "everything happens for a reason". For this reason I always tell young budding footballers this "never put all your hopes in your legs when you have a head!" Focus on what you can do and have football as a pastime and if you make it, great!

"My hindsight was now offered as foresight."

One man's loss is another man's gain...

Even though these aspects in my life were not realised, I found these experiences in my new found career to be invaluable gold dust that now won the hearts of new admirers... the mentees. It was the stuff folklore was made out of and it was like telling old war stories around a camp fire at night with hot dogs, as I shared my football and music exploits with students who were considered hard to engage who were now fully engaged. My pain and past disappointments in life now became direction and correction for those I was working with. My hindsight was now offered as foresight and because I had the emotional and mental war scars and abilities to prove it, they were won forever! Now my 10,000 hours was no longer in context with my history and confined to my past, but now had great relevance in my present as my experience enabled me to guide those who were making those kind of decisions now. I had now gained a level of respect that could not be achieved from having a predominantly theoretical standpoint! I have found young people to be truly authentic, sincere, honest and for them to be won they needed to hear, see and feel authenticity.

Nothing is new under the sun, just repackaged!

This had now opened up a new chapter in the book of Herman Stewart because I could now use my experiences that I thought would be lost due to the dramatic change of industry and career choice, to further the experiences and value of young people within my care. I would share tips, insights and wisdom only attained by years of practise, pain and preparation, which the young people listened to and accepted. I also saw in the music that they had an interest in, something different which was new and fresh. A form of expression I was not totally familiar with but very acquainted to. As they shared their musical tastes, that was edgy, urban and of course; stylistic. Once again, I was in my element, a new element with a new perspective but an old appreciation! My loss was now gain, my years of pain, confusion, frustration and inner turmoil were now a comfort and reassurance to me. It's amazing how things can change. But we must change first. I was now glad I had walked instead of waiting at the bus stop...

Get your ticket!

In the school I was now in charge of the DJ workshop which was more of a role of facilitation. We had a DJ come in named Jason who would help the students to learn how to use the decks and make beats. However, this was not a given but a privilege that after only a few sessions was about to go through some rigorous regulation. As a part of the programme, for the students to access the DJ sessions they had to be up to date with their school work or be willing to attend homework club (which I ran) to catch up before the next session. Also they were to avoid being in any form of trouble within the school, if they wanted to attend or participate. Now this was alien, tough and somewhat unfair to many of the students especially those who ran into trouble consistently! But they were needed guidelines to guard the provision and boundaries given as an incentive to ensure the school's investment was not counterproductive.

"They were slick and determined."

Before every session I would personally give the students the tickets which would sort the wheat from the chaff! Due to the fact I was in contact with most staff, I would have been made aware of issues regarding any trouble or any issues of outstanding coursework etc. I guess the new relationship reinvention that was so necessary during the holiday was very timely because I was soon to be in the bad books of some students, which would have been previously more awkward. We even had circumstances where students were getting tickets from the black market as some students who were being entrepreneurial after spotting a gap in the market they started reproducing counterfeit tickets! What a cheek. Never doubt the ability and potential of these students, I mean they were slick and determined because some who were not allowed to attend due to breaking the agreement of producing work and exemplary behavior, would even come and negotiate at the door with me to see if they could get in! This never worked. For this reason, I was not the favourite member of staff for many so my newly orchestrated distance was very necessary.

I am going to stop DJ workshop!

I was very fortunate as we had a very innovative head teacher in Mr David Brown. I am telling you he had a passion for young people and a vision. But, he also never messed about! I remember for some reason he felt he was not getting a return on investment concerning this DJ coming in to school to work with the young people, due to the fact some of the boys were still messing about and sometimes when they messed about, they really messed about! I cannot remember what the trigger was but for some reason the Head approached me and told me to tell the boys that the DJ workshop was going to be stopped. This was quite dramatic because the head was encouraging this provision to be delivered and could see that some improvements had been made by the students however, he felt there was not enough (or he was using his Cambridge educated psychology on us all).

The mediator

As requested, I went and told the boys that the DJ provision was going to be stopped. As expected they were disgruntled, heckling, disputing but deep down they were gutted! And I felt it for them. These guys were talented, in fact very talented and loved the release that these sessions and the form of creative therapy offered, especially in school time. You see during school with all the expectations, stresses, challenge management necessary due to varying relationships with teachers and some peers who got on their nerves, this session was a God send to help focus their energies. Personally, I could see the benefits of them taking part in these sessions because after all, I was the ticket holder so I knew. The regime was hardnosed, any bad behaviour or lack of homework completed equalled no DJ workshop! It was a hard line but the power was used and leveraged for their benefit and the principle was paramount not their feelings. So after hearing a few moans and "that's not fair's" I agreed with them and told them that I would go back to the Head.

Rock in a hard place

After bringing the message on behalf of the Head it was now his turn to be the receiver of a message. I brought their message of groans to him and then started to negotiate on their behalf. It was like negotiating for pay but, not in a monetary sense. But Mr Brown and I knew what it meant to negotiate as we had done it for some time and there was a time when we negotiated for the good part of a week before conclusion. So he knew my style and I knew his... hard! To paint a picture, it was like we were formidable foes in those old school kung fu movies but at the same time respectful and wary of each other's personal style, leadership and work. So I cut to the chase and started speaking about the provision of the DJ coming in and the response that the young people gave when I was the bearer of bad news. He was understanding of where they were coming from but then shared his concerns then I shared mine as the advocate for young freedom of expression and its benefits from my perspective. We then came to a common understanding of a way forward. So this is what the requirement was, if the Head was to continue bank rolling the DJ to come in, the students would now have to write a letter that would express why they wanted the DJ workshop to continue and what they were prepared to do for its continuation. The boys were up for the letter writing challenge laid down by the Head.

Bad news was not so bad after all...

So I had to meet with the boys again and make them aware of Mr Brown's response and his requirements to continue the sessions. As I shared the expectations some of the students had a glint in their eyes as if they knew that his requirements were highly achievable, whilst others responded "that's long" which in street speak means "long winded and unnecessary" but more or less, everyone was prepared to make it happen. So now this letter had to be written and I had volunteered to help them articulate the letter in teacher speak (the language and phraseology of educators) but in their words. As we wrote this letter, as they started to justify why they should have DJ workshop, I started to see how they were learning language and literacy through writing street hymns aka rhymes and performing them publically. By the extended use of vocabulary that they would use to show their lyrical dexterity and verbal prowess in their search for new words was extending their verbal command and the use of English language and literature. This was also shown in how they structured the verses in their songs which was a grammatical exercise (for the good or bad). It was also identified that due to them performing over musical backgrounds they had to gain an understanding of bars, notes, the length of notes and the purpose of a metronome (a timing instrument) that helps the 1,2,3,4 -1,2,3,4. Clearly, this process of measurement is mathematical, so the core skills of English and Maths was being utilised during the sessions and was being expressed in the letter. They also noted the performance aspect which has its own impact on self esteem as it increases confidence to speak publically and the whole notion of being important enough to have something to say! Which children seldom believe. So with all said and done they compiled an excellent letter that stated not only the academic benefits but also the personal value added as the overall return of investment for the school as the behaviour and work completion element was still intact.

"Would he continue the provision?"

Would he be convinced? Would he reverse his thoughts and extend the provision? And have a greater appreciation for what the young people were doing? This was more than recreational but also an informal education tool. These questions could not be answered without another encounter with my formidable foe (well you know what I mean...). When I met him and handed over their letter he was pleased and it seemed he had achieved his objective of them having a greater appreciation of the privilege, for that's what it was. I am sure he also had a greater appreciation of the fringe benefits of the learning that was taking place whilst they participated in the DJ workshop. He continued the provision which was truly a good thing, as they were entered into a city wide audition to find the best school and we were recognised as one of the best within the City! Not only that the boys represented the school at the CBSO in front of some distinguished folk and raised their profile as well as the school's.

Football, football, football

Talk about "don't call it a comeback, I've been here for years" which was the first line taken from LL Cool J's "Mama Said knock 'em out" single, I was approached by a member of the Physical Education department as they wanted some support to help coach the school football teams. They were aware of my previous football history (in staff games they got a glimpse) and asked if I could manage one of the years. After a discussion, I thought it would be a good opportunity to connect the dots by coaching the year 11 team who I was mentoring as well. But boy did I have a new challenge on my hands....

The first team talk...

It was lunchtime and our place of gathering was in an English classroom that I had borrowed for this occasion. I made all the team aware that we needed to talk. Some players took longer to arrive as it was lunchtime and they got magnetised by the school community and the scent of the canteen whilst others were there on time eager with anticipation, to hear what I had to share. The time had arrived as I looked at them many stared at me with bewilderment as to why I had called this meeting. So when all were finally present, I shared the news that I was now their new football manager! It was very encouraging as the news was greeted with smiles, nods and many affirmations to my delight. I also sensed a seriousness and belief that we could achieve something great together, the sky was the limit and I was not wishy washy or fluffy in any manner. As I desired that we start as we mean to go on, I firmly stated the standards would be high and we would achieve great things but not without the cost of commitment, sacrifice and effort. I believe they were convinced and I guess the respect they had for me knowing my history, carried much weight. The players recognised I was serious and that I was not about to make familiarity hinder the progress that we were able to make. So to conclude the meeting, I made the players aware that no-one's place was safe in the team regardless of the past and that I would offer everyone a chance to prove their desire, team worth and passion. I vehemently made all aware I was more interested in the players who were teachable and willing to learn, who had the right attitude even if their ability was not exemplary, over the players who had much skill and ability but never had the humility to listen to instructions because of their puffed up sense of self. And I had my personal reasons for such requirements because being so close to success but so far because of a misguided attitude was something that I had personally experienced and suffered from in my football days.

Football is not a given but a privilege!

As I flashback to when I was in school, I truly felt I was the "special one" like Jose *Mourinho* when it came to football. This really affected me a lot because I never truly applied myself to academic studies because I "was" going to become a pro footballer. This blinkered attitude was one of my greatest hindrances, because I would not heed wise counsel even from those who knew more than me. This included my PE teacher Mr. Davis who was an ex-professional footballer, such pigheadedness was bound to be my downfall. But, I just loved football! And in school, it was one of the only things that made me tick. In reflection, most of my fondest school memories included a football in fact, any ball! We even played with tennis balls, footballs, netballs in general; any ball we could get our hands on. So I knew and understood what I was on about when I shared my requirements with my new team. I knew from my personal experience of football's potential to distract students from the main reason why they are in school, which can be disastrous! I even remember some teachers knew football was my Achilles heel, so if I never done my school work or acted up in lesson; I would be stopped from attending football training and even banned from playing football matches, which was not fair! But got my attention. So with my first hand experience of the negative impact an undisciplined passion for football can have on a student, I could not leave it to chance. So from the offset; I set out to correct some of my past wrongs, by creating the right perspective and perimeters for the players in the team. Whether they liked it or not… at least my hindsight could now become their foresight and my past pain, their present gain.

"It was one of the only things that made me tick."

You're not fair!

From the get go, I laid some solid boundaries and expectations as their coach that was as follows:

1. They would attend consistently and on time to all training sessions and would not be included in matches if they were not present, unless they had acceptable reasons.

2. I would expect that their school work would be completed and would always take precedence over their sporting activity and if this was not the case, they were at risk of not being included and

3. They would respect me as a person and their coach and I would not be taking any slack regardless of who they are. So if their attitude, conduct or application was not right then sadly their football participation within this team would be short lived.

As you can imagine these standards were not enthusiastically accepted by all but they were agreed as a principle and respected, bottom line. This is what's needed as young people desire boundaries that are consistent and communicated effectively which are firm but fair. When we do not present such clear guidelines that are understood the lines become blurred and it just creates room for gray areas and then compromise, which always weakens someone's message.

On many occasions, I have witnessed the aspirations that a lot of students especially young African Caribbean boys entertain are either sports or entertainment such as music. I know this could be considered the pot calling the kettle black as I have pursued both the aforementioned careers, however my choices were based on the knowledge I had then and I never had much mentoring and wise career advice early enough which could have helped broaden my horizons. Now I know and understand because of being a prime example that many young black boys have a natural aptitude to be exemplary in both fields, however I believe that we could be much more and they that have the potential need to be much more. For years I have seen young players place their life's hope in their legs instead of in their heads! And I have mentored a number of players who were signed up for premiership teams during their secondary education and have taken school and playing for such a pristine team for granted. Then in a sad turn of fate, I have seen many of these teams not give them a professional contract at the expected age of 16 to their horror! And with nowhere else to turn as they never had a plan B and some even lacking the ability to reinvent themselves or the resilience to persist in another discipline, many then go on to attain the meandering heights of mediocrity! This is painful as they were always able to, plus born to achieve more.

"This is painful as they were always able to, plus born to achieve more."

I have mentioned black boys in this example but it also goes across the board where out of low self esteem, misinformation or laziness many accept less than they are worth! And this was not my desire for this team. You can call me Coach Carter the 2nd, every player was to have a dream that was bigger than football and they were to have options just in case football never became a professional career! As every football player is one game away from a career ending tackle or injury (I had a repetitive groin injury which never helped). So if you know anyone who fits this profile please share this train of thought with them so they don't *just* follow the dream of being a footballer, but continue playing football passionately as a hobby and have something that they could have "some" control over achieving i.e. a career plan, an apprenticeship or structured further/higher education (3 years then qualification). As you see you do not choose being a footballer someone chooses (scouts) you so don't just wait for that someone else! And if on the way to achieving that career goal or educational aspiration, football (whilst a hobby) takes off, then go with it! But even if it does not, you can still enjoy playing your passion, week in week out as a semi pro in Saturday or Sunday league and still provide for you and your family. Take it from me, I know what I am talking about...

allow my pain to be your gain!

So the regime was hard, the bar was set high, my expectations were not realistic but it worked! They would attend after school practise and put their hearts in and those who had attitudes toned them down for the love of the game (at least, their love of being able to play the game in this team!).

Mentee case study: Makindi Konwandi

CS

In secondary school I would say I was mischievous like all boys are at times, but at that point in my life, it was a very important stage for me in school. My exams were approaching; I was more focused on girls and other stuff, rather than books and my education. I was always able to do the work but was not fulfilling my full potential. I was getting caught up in a lot of things that didn't concern me, but because of the people I 'rolled' with or the type of person I am I was always labelled. Getting labelled is not a nice feeling, especially if it's not you but it's the feeling of looking like an outsider with your peers.

I can remember the day in school, when my HOY came to my form and took me to her office. On the way to her office, all sorts of things were going through my mind but not once did mentoring run through it. When she initially told me I was going to start seeing a mentor, I didn't know what to think but I was hearing a lot about mentoring floating around within school. At first, I was very apprehensive as to why I would need mentoring and what for. Once I met the mentor and we had a meeting he told me what he expected from me and also what I expected from him if the relationship was too work. It was sort of like as if a new friendship/relationship had been formed without me even taking much attention to this at that stage. As the sessions began to progress and I would see the mentor almost everywhere in the school, I also used to hear his voice in my head during lessons saying "Come on, do your best, you know you can do it! Only a few more months left and your school life will be done".

Not once did I feel the mentor listened or stereotyped me in his views and opinions of me. He always had the best intentions for me and my education in and out of school. We would talk about a vast number of things during our sessions, gaining a lot of knowledge from his experiences through his life and the skills he was willing to share. He was seen as a teacher figure but more as our teacher / mediator. He would negotiate with me and teachers to smooth out any problems which were encountered within school. He was willing to relate to me on a personal level, valuing my opinion and making me not see things from one perspective but to look at the bigger picture. My relationship with the teachers dramatically changed after I had spoken to them. We shared our opinions and concerns whilst in the presence of the mentor. They would see me in the corridors or around the school and would stop and talk to me, but not telling me off but asking if I needed any extra help in their lessons or with any work I had. I was beginning to pay more attention to the detail of my work especially in art and graphics.

Mentoring really helped me because it made me have someone there to talk to within school about absolutely anything. To have your opinion always valued and to feel welcomed to speak is always a good thing to have around you when growing up. Someone who is always willing to let you know experiences they had in their life whether good or bad is a key to guiding someone to choose whether they take it on board and acknowledge this. Using the skills I gained and the impact mentoring had on me I went to college and studied it. I now work with children in primary and secondary schools. I have a strong passion for the work I do because the impact it can have on changing a child's life is very beneficial and words cannot express the feeling it gives. I have been mentoring now for a number of years, also working in the school I once attended as a pupil.

The bust up!

I remember one training session we were preparing for a game and as a team we were really progressing in the league and cup so there was pressure, however I was not letting up. And during training I was asking of the team to do certain drills to simply strive for excellence. Something happened where I demanded more effort from one of my players and he just blew! And he was ranting and going off disrespecting me in front of the team and I blew also! And this guy was big! But he could have been "big little more" (which is Patois for 'I don't care') as I'm the Manager. So I just sent him away to get changed which he was doing anyway and I told him he can forget about playing the game and he was acting like he didn't care anyway! All the other players were present and this just did not look good. And to make it worse he was one of my top players and was always dependable to play a solid game at the back. Anyway, a day later he came up to me and apologised for his behaviour and we made amends and he was back in the team and everything was back on track. The other players were glad as he was such a rock for the team and irreversibly one of the "mans". After our episode our relationship became stronger and we both had a greater insight into how we should deal with each other and also the team had seen that I was not going to compromise even if they were a good player. In my books, no one was indispensable and even if that meant we had to lose the cup to prove it, the principle must stand or else everything we stood for falls!

It was all worth it...

So we worked hard as a team, they played hard and as a unit, we laughed hard and enjoyed the fruits of our labour which was success. Game after game we progressed and it was duly noted as on a regular basis it was mentioned in the staff briefing that we were advancing and making the school proud! I was also promised by the Head that he would buy me a pint if we won the cup which was good of him. The penultimate game was here and we were at the verge of achieving great things because our next game was for the cup. We played this game against Holyhead who were a local rival, and we won confidently. We had also secured top place in the league so as my first season as the Manager we had won the double! And the first time in the team's history! So we did achieve great things but above all we achieved respect, understanding as well as a new personal value. My year 11 team seriously did me proud and this was the same group that many had laughed at me for mentoring. This group of young people taught me a lot, they taught me that anyone can change and achieve beyond their present performance if given the right support, help, encouragement and guidance. This group of players had made history during their last year, considered the last bite of the cherry, they really did me proud and I feel emotional as I type this as I consider how we all overcame adversity to experience success together. Never let anyone tell you or judge you in a way that prevents you from trying to do what is in your heart to do. It is important that you do not let the challenges, obstacles or the opinions of others stop you because you can do it!

So we did achieve great things but above all we achieved respect, understanding as well as a new personal value

A great way to say goodbye...

Not only did they achieve great things on the pitch they also all completed their school career without any of my group of 15 mentees being permanently excluded. Most of mentees left the school with good grades, significantly breaking the national trend of "Black boy" underachievement with over 50% of my group achieving 5+ GCSE C and above marks. Football was now paying off and I had learnt how to make all things work for the good, even with what first was seemingly bad! This was my pay off for all that I had gone through that was not as fruitful as I would have liked it to have been. I could see that all things can become good even if it was not in the first instance. All the disappointments, frustrations, inner tears and fears of not being able to articulate my value and vision were all now subsiding as I was seeing that everything that I was touching was turning to success and silencing the little voices that for years have desired my demise (as well as the external naysayers). Just thinking of the members of staff who laughed at the impossibility of my task which was not necessarily encouraging, but in an ironic way, helped to propel me forward. If you know me you know challenge fuels me as I am a fighter, a warrior and my life had prepared me to encounter such challenges and overcome them because it was what I had to do, to be where I was now.

Some of my mentees have gone on to be mentors also and help the younger generation which has been a real blessing to me and I just want to encourage you to make sure you do not short change yourself, go for your goals even though in the first instance they may be seriously intimidating, but know that within you is greatness, a winner and adversity can become the wind behind your sails to push you forward. It all depends on you and your attitude!

Activity – All things work for the good

1. What area of your life have you invested your 10,000 hours in? And what activities have you done to do so?

2. Is it in the area that you are currently operating in?

3. How positive are you concerning you and your life?

4. How healthy are the conversations that you have with yourself in your head?

The Cry for Mentoring

The Good the Bad and the Mentoring

From my first experiences of mentoring within school and the young people that I had to mentor, it was quickly setting a trend that never sat well with me. Even though I was mentoring and every life is important regardless of their background, circumstances, ability or lack of it, there was still a disturbing pattern evolving that I never truly agreed with, even though it gave me joy to address. The truth is that not everything is really politically correct and many things are spoken of undiplomatically. Reason being, if you say some things "as they are" some truths or the truth of some situations, are unequivocally wrong! I say all this to address: why is mentoring within education predominantly viewed as it is? You may question how is it viewed? Well let's continue...

"Some truths or the truth of some situations, are unequivocally wrong!"

For those who work within education, what type of student do you perceive needs mentoring? It may be politically correct to have an all inclusive view on this matter, but I ask that you take a moment and consider the following questions: Should mentoring be for:

(A) The bright and self motivated students that can get along with their own work regardless of being supported?

(B) The student who suffers with low self esteem, image and confidence issues?

(C) The student who is experiencing the upheavals of parental separation or other personal issues that life just happens to bring their way, regardless of your academic ability? Or

(D) Students who behave badly within school who are hard to contain within a classroom setting and are preventing others from learning?

What would your answer of been without having the options before you? Due to my years of hands on mentoring experience with a multitude of face to face discussions with students, the only correct answer can be all of the above because they could be mentored for different reasons. However, most mentoring models on a national scale predominantly lean towards answer D! Which is not fair as every child needs a mentor not only those who have challenging behaviour even though their need at times is a priority.

What makes you say that?

When I first started mentoring within the education sector in 2001 there was a national issue first and foremost with "Black boy" underachievement. This was seen as an educational and social issue where a lot of "Black boys" were being misunderstood and it was also highlighted that this could be a result of the shortage of positive male intervention due to an absence of some fathers. Due to the data and the apparent issues these young people were also labelled as at risk of social exclusion, considered hard to reach, hard to engage and disinterested (what a bunch of negative labels!). So as an initiative, mentoring was being used to combat this phenomena to raise standards and to engage young people that were slipping through the net and suffering from school disengagement, low attendance, poor punctuality, under achievement and poor behaviour. As a principle it was noteworthy hence it receiving the level of support and national resource to address plus the need was there. However, this model would then create its own self fulfilling prophesy which I personally experienced and disagreed with.

I want to mentor more than just black children!

This may seem so contradictory and controversial and even traitorous. However there is a method to my madness! From the start of my mentoring career I was referred "Black boy" after "Black boy" to mentor, which I never had a problem with and was glad to support those that needed my support. I saw myself in them and observed that many of these boys needed a dose of masculine challenge and someone who could emphatically tell them to "fix up" (which means to correct yourself and improve sharply!). I had cultural empathy, community understanding, social and emotional intelligence plus a level of experience that made me authentic in their eyes; it enabled my work to work. I was successful for many reasons not just because "I is Black" as Ali G would retort, but because I could understand young people and also communicate that understanding in a way that was conducive to school. Time after time, I have seen young people turn around and become better students not because I made them better, but because it was in them and I just helped to facilitate that directional movement from under performance to greater performance, so my mentoring was working.

"I was successful for many reasons not just because "I is Black" as Ali G would retort."

So what was the problem?

The more I was mentoring "Black boys" who were deemed to be "naughty" the more I was observing that they were becoming stigmatised because they had a mentor. And the perception of mentoring in school at that time (and it still is in many schools within the UK) was contributing to this self fulfilling prophesy and needed to change! So imagine, if I am just mentoring "Black boys" and my mentoring list had no other ethnicity on it, what would that be saying about "Black boys" and inadvertently, the service I was providing? Unfortunately it would be saying that only "Black boys" needed mentoring which was totally untrue. However, mentoring was shaping up in this way because I could identify a number of other children who could have benefitted from it, who were not being mentored.

Some may say 'I do not have black boys within my school', which is true in many cases but, regardless of the ethnicity of your learning community, I invite you to answer the following questions:

- What is the profile of your typical mentee within your mentoring database?

- What is the most prevalent reason why your students are mentored?

- What type of student does your mentoring programme focus most of its resources on?

- Where is your mentoring provision positioned within your organisation and within the School Improvement Plan?

- Is your mentoring provision attached to the behaviour unit, inclusion or a consequence system?

- How are your mentees identified and referred? Is it in any way connected to internal or external exclusion or any other punitive measure?

If the profile of your mentees on the mentoring provision are viewed as naughty; your programme has a high possibility of strategically or unconsciously encouraging a counterproductive mentoring culture. There is also a high possibility that your school's teaching and learning community's perception will be that mentoring "is" for naughty children.

And to tell the truth, how and why would they think any different? When your organisation has systematically endorsed this practise by reinforcing this punitive approach to mentoring (we will talk more about this later book).

"Can you mentor me?"

The showdown

I had come to my conclusion and had decided, I no longer wanted to deliver my work "exclusively" to black boys. I thoroughly enjoyed mentoring the young boys who were Black, I understood their plight, had cultural empathy and a great affinity with also. Due to mentoring the boys and being respected, I had already gained the buy in from the most influential pupils in the school who were leaders and highly talented in their own right (one of my mentees gained an A* in a GCSE subject from year 10!). However, whilst going about my business within the school, I was building relationships with students from all backgrounds who at some point would ask me the golden question... "Can you mentor me?" This question bugged me and also made me think, why can I not mentor the others? This was compounded by the fact that when I was having mentoring sessions and doing my explorative Colombo work via informal mentoring sessions in the playground or where students would approach me, I was discovering or unravelling a lot of the issues that the pupils were experiencing were not exclusive to any single ethnicity but was transferable due to the nature of the concerns. Most of the students I was speaking to were experiencing emotional (anger, fear, frustration), mental (anxiety, worry and confusion) personal (social/home) and spiritual issues (low self esteem, identity, self image, confidence and self belief). For this reason, I felt things weren't right, so I arranged to see the Head.

It's not fair!

The bottom line was, I did not want to be one of the reasons why these young "Black boys" were being further stereotyped, which I knew was happening. Due to the perception of mentoring being a solution for behaviour, the more that I saw the boys, the more they were being stigmatised.

As I flashed back I remembered when my mum commended me and she shared how she observed that from a young age I had a eclectic mix of friendships with boys and girls from different races, as I brought home many friends from different cultures. So developing a variety of relationships was not an issue and in a sense was something that I wanted to do. I felt this because the service that was being provided could be of benefit to as many people as possible which would be great, plus would create a greater scope of my competencies as a practitioner. My previous eclectic experience, even from primary school was now a significant part of my arsenal, as I had the ability to understand others, so with this in mind and my new purpose for mentoring being for all students, so I approached the Head.

Equal opportunities

My Head teacher was visionary and quite on the button and also saw the connection between pastoral imbalances and academic achievement. He understood that academia and pastoral issues could not be divorced but affected each other and for some to create equilibrium in their present circumstances, more than academia was needed. So I never had problems speaking to him or sharing my heart on such matters, as he sincerely desired to support young people holistically. I just made my case known concerning the fact that I didn't feel the school's present mentoring provision accommodated all children, so to me it was unethical due to not totally adhering equal opportunities. I had to be careful here and not take for granted the fact that the school was doing good by these boys who needed additional support that was unique to them. We were both aware that the mentoring provision was doing well by creating a level playing field for those who were struggling to access the curriculum and adjusting to the realities in school. So it was already addressing inequalities that existed, such as the need for healthy teacher - pupil relationships etc. However, only a few were able to access the support provided by mentoring due to the current mentoring mandate and organisational purpose of the provision and that was the problem. Plus all of this was reiterated by the embedded referral system.

"I believe every child should have access to mentoring support."

Through our conversation, I made David Brown, our Head teacher, aware of the different types of children that were approaching me for mentoring and I also shared as a professional that I did not desire to become pigeonholed as only being able to work with "Black boys". Also I felt that by predominately mentoring African Caribbean boys it was presenting another problem which would make them vulnerable to opportunities of being stigmatised again. Because if mentoring was only deemed for "Black boys" and the "Black boys" who were mentored were predominantly supported for behavioural issues then this would send a message that mentoring was for "Black boys" with behaviour problems which is not politically correct or ethical.

The other predicament that we would have is the programme could give off a message that "Black boys" need mentoring to behave "normally" so now they would become special in a different way, which would create another form of stigma. Also I believed I was a professional practitioner in my own right and could not be fobbed off for just being able to connect with those from my background when it came to me having to represent my mentees or be an advocate for them. This "Black boy" exclusivity approach could have less credence and credibility, so I would be less effective for those who I supported. So here were my dilemmas. After this conversation he agreed with what I shared and I was then able to at least take the first step to creating mentoring inclusivity.

Escaping the stigma

I believe every child should have access to mentoring support within school regardless of whatever you call the provision; academic or pastoral because all pupils are people and come to school with a life and context attached to them. Due to this fact, it is very possible that they will come with a barrage of needs that go beyond academic teaching and learning. And a lot of these young people in particular would need their concerns to be addressed before they can effectively be "ready to learn" or able to successfully access the curriculum. On a personal level, I view children as adults who just have not grown up or developed yet, which they are. I see pupils as people and not just a potential 5 A-C's or solely an opportunity for a school to advance up the school league table due to extra points because of greater whole school attainment. I know that this is a part of the package, but I am a firm believer of, since schools exercise loco parentis (being the child's parent) whilst the child is within their care, it is laudable for schools to also embrace their moral obligation to develop children holistically. Even though a school has its limitations because the school is only exercising loco parentis but, are not the real parents. However, a child can see their school and teachers more than their own home and parents especially when some parents are working all the hours that God sends to make ends. So it should count for something. Also this is not helped by children being in their rooms on Facebook, BB-ing, X –Box or in front of television or a games console instead of spending time in the same room as their parents, never mind quality time, which is sad.

"Mentoring cannot just be for one type of child."

The reality of it is when a child is not in school they are experiencing life in a variety of ways and when they come to school many just act out how they are experiencing life. For some, things are fine at home but still have a tendency to behave like it is otherwise. However, I have seen pupils who are experiencing horrendous lives at home and they behave like everything is alright. The point is many children come to school and because of what they are exposed to i.e. seeing, hearing or feeling at home, when they are in school they are not necessarily in the right frame of mind to access the education that is provided for them. In these cases mentoring is an invaluable tool as the mentee has the opportunity to speak to someone who can be a pair of ears and a captive audience which enables the young person to share, vent or express how they are feeling in a healthy environment and receive guidance, support and access to a sounding board whilst they are processing and learning how to manage, cope or accept what they are going through. This is why I believe mentoring cannot just be for one type of child, ethnicity, gender or age as all people need support as life presents challenges to us all which many a time we need additional support to get us through. So I am sure you are starting to see the variety of problems a biased and negatively viewed mentoring programme can present.

My child is not going to be mentored

On a number of occasions, I have had to be "on the front line" and be the one who contacts the parent to make them aware that their child has been identified as to needing mentoring support. And boy this has presented me with a few challenges. On a regular basis, I would come up against some serious resistance from determined parents, convinced that mentoring was not the way forward for their child. And in many cases they would sternly say their child would not be mentored, which I respected, but never accepted and would persist to bring clarity concerning what I "mean" by mentoring. And I would speak to all these parents and I would listen to their concerns and at times be the recipient of their venting opportunity as the face or voice of the school but, all in all we would arrive at a place of common respect, understanding and perspective. However, the conversation would go something like this:

Me: "Hello my name is Herman Stewart and I am calling from Hamstead Hall and I would like to make you aware that it has been identified that your child could potentially benefit from being mentored" is it something you would be interested in them receiving?

Parent: "Ok is there something wrong? Why does my child need mentoring?"

Me: "No I am not saying there is something wrong, it is just something the HoY believes would be of great benefit to support your child in school "

Parent:"But if he is doing alright, why does he need a mentor? No I don't want my child to be mentored because mentoring is for naughty children"

Me "No, not really, at this school mentoring is for all children who could do with additional support to achieve their best. For some students just to be able to have another member of staff working with them besides a teacher has helped significantly. I personally mentor young people for a variety of reasons that have nothing to do with behaviour. The reasons can vary from building confidence, motivational, organisational skills, bullying as well as behaviour, it is all about getting the best for your child and this would help".

After a few moments of going back and forth with the parent, we would come to an understanding that ultimately, we wanted the same thing... the best for their child. And as we were in school, we were able to engage with the child on another level so it could only be good. Which was mostly agreed and I am not saying all parents were like the parent in the conversation but this is an example of something that was quite common. But why did I have to go through all that before the parent would understand and not be as resistant to the idea of their child gaining additional support? Here is part of the answer.

The bigger problem...

When mentoring was introduced to the masses as an intervention to raise standards and address underachievement, this is where it all started. Even though I must credit the government at the time (Labour) with the introduction of mentors into education via the Excellence in Cities initiative, the initiative was great but the way that the mentoring strategy was implemented was what created the problem. Now let me explain: When mentoring was introduced into schools at the end of the 1990s, the remit or those that it was aimed at supporting were the pupils who were suffering from low attendance, poor punctuality and were experiencing social exclusion and some were even classed as "disengaged" or "disinterested". In other terms they were not having a healthy social or educational experience. The introduction of mentors into school was a part of the solution as they could work in a way that conventional school staff couldn't. And in some circles, mentoring was seen as a remedy to the absent father deficit that was experienced in the black community and a way of "replacing" the father with a role model of an older man to a younger man because in many cases that role model was not present. However this caused many problems in itself, which I was experiencing in the early days of my career. You see this concept was laudable but quite short sighted that an educational role could or would plug such a vast social or community gap so the expectation was commendable, ambitious but unrealistic.

This also affected how mentors and mentees were viewed by teachers, staff, parents and the mentees themselves. The provision was created to address specific issues and was successful at doing so, however, the perception of mentors was not always favourable due to the informality of their approach and the relationships they were able to develop with the students. In some instances some teachers and some mentors never saw eye to eye which was detrimental to all involved with some mentors being kept out of the loop and even isolated from the inner circle of influential teachers. As a result many students were now being stigmatised by being mentored because the programmes that many schools adopted was based on the "deficit model" which meant something had to be wrong or failing for you to qualify to be mentored. For some schools this approach may be a thing of the past but sadly this is an entrenched practise and is very much alive in many schools in the UK.

R **Reflection:** If this practise were to continue it would seriously undermine the benefits and potential that mentoring could provide for ALL students. This is not an aspirant mentoring approach so it would rarely touch the students in a school that truly need the support.

"Clearly there are good and poor mentors."

You can't handle the truth! This has got to be one of the most repeated lines by Jack Nicholson who was playing the part of an officer of high rank in the army, in the movie "A Few Good Men". The scene I am referring to, Jack was under oath and being questioned by Tom Cruise who was playing his opposite. After Jack was being grilled in the stand he got to the point where he just shouted "You cannot handle the truth!", which on many fronts in true life I totally agree. You see the truth can be bitter but, it is usually better that the truth be known. That's how I feel about mentoring in education. The initiative was truly inspired and to me is clearly one of the most innovative roles that have been introduced to the education system. And is one of the most relevant when it comes to addressing societal changes and the holistic needs of the students. However, it has been misused, abused, misunderstood and demeaned. Mentoring has not been regarded as a profession but a role which has been berated. Clearly there are good and poor mentors, and sometimes many mentors are tarred with the same brush. So taking this into account there must be skill, talent, intuition, insight and even mastery involved, if you can differentiate on a competency level. But mentors have been viewed in some schools as school security guards, professional baby sitters, or the dog's body. So the most relevant question is not what do you do as a mentor but, in most cases it is more like, what don't you do?

How can you say that?

Many schools, and please note me here not *all*, use mentoring as a behaviour management strategy. Mentors in their most abased role are denigrated to containment and the isolation of students to administer punishment for other staff who simply do not have the time or the will to do so. You may say this sounds so primitive but this is happening and I could introduce you to mentors who could verify these claims. No wonder some parents refuse point blank such support (if you can call it that) even though this is not what I consider to be mentoring.

What I consider to be mentoring is: a professional informal relationship that enables both mentee and mentor to be further developed as people and learners. It is used to encourage problem solving, creative thinking, and increased performance so the mentee can experience their potential. It is bespoke and individual; aspirant highly sought after and is invaluable to many who benefit from the dynamic personal development instrument that it is (when used positively).

Twinkle in the eye, that glint of hope...

Just to see a glint in the eye of a student who had just experienced that life defining "Aha" moment, when the penny had dropped during a mentoring session. These moments are priceless and they are what TRUE mentors seek. When used in this way mentoring adds a powerful dynamic to the overall school operation because the sheer manoeuvrability a well positioned mentor offers can only be good for the learning and wider community. As they connect school, community, external agencies, parents and the mentee. When used most effectively, mentors can be compared to a good Common Assessment Framework (CAF) Lead Practitioner, as they marry all interested in the child's progression together by being the link to the pupil, once they have the right kind of relationship. As mentoring is relational the stronger the relationship the more can be achieved via the intervention.

I believe all children should "at least" have the opportunity to access a significant adult who is able to facilitate a mentoring relationship for the benefit of the young person's development. This could only be good and not only benefit the school's attainment but also add personal value to the student as an individual. My question is, why do we have to view mentoring like this within education? After all, in other fields mentors are venerated and well sought after whether it is sports, business, music or any other professional arena, mentoring is well respected and appreciated. And so it should be in mainstream schools.

 Seven tips to a recession proof mentoring programme

1. All that you need is within you. This is the same for some aspects of your staffing - find the talent and maximise them.

2. Where are your leaders among you? Identify the students that could lead a tribe for the school.

3. Change your perception of mentoring to ensure that it is viewed as a positive intervention.

4. Create preventative mentoring approaches so less time is spent on fire fighting and wasting resources on crisis management.

5. View mentoring strategically so all resources can be allocated effectively and the right type of mentoring can be distributed at the right time.

6. Be honest and address what is not working quickly so there is less time, resource and human potential wasted.

7. Recognise that your mentoring programme will only be as innovative and effective as its leader so appoint appropriately. It can be more costly to save money in many circumstances.

"Mentoring is relational so the stronger the relationship the more can be achieved."

True Education is more than Academia

What I have found for years whether a general consensus or simply my observation, there seems to be an assumption that socially by the time that young people are within school especially secondary school that they should have an understanding of social etiquette and appropriate social behaviour. However, this could not be any further from the truth. You see the reality is a lot of parents found school challenging and some also had a challenging up-bringing and through no fault of their own may not have attained all the necessary life and social skills that are then required for successful social interaction which poses its own challenges. My question is "How do you impart what you do not have?" How can you give to your offspring what you have not gained yet? You cannot give what you do not have and a lot of parents are in this category. Being a parent I see I am limited in my own capabilities as a person and find it difficult helping my 12 year old daughter with some mathematical equations that I did not master myself or simply I was not present in that lesson. And looking at what is expected from us nowadays even just taking a look on the economical aspect families are challenged more than ever. Before, it was probably more viable or even an option that one parent could stay at home while one could work as the other cared for and raised the children but with the cost of living and inflation rising and pay increases frozen, there is now a situation that parents are having to work all the days that God sends, to make ends meet. And even if they are around, preoccupation is the new meditation as they work out using mental arithmetic how they are going to get to the end of the month. Very present in body but not so present in mind these parents would be considering... How are the bills going to be paid? Children fed? Clothes brought? And rent/mortgage paid? The challenge escalates up a notch, especially if the parent doing the calculating is the sole provider in their family.

So who is bringing up the kids?

Scary as it may be but, the new parent, educator or baby sitter is the TV. It could also be a game console, the social media or friends who are more than willing to give advice but, are still yet to gain a sound understanding of life, which their years do not yet afford them. So children, not all but some, are being brought up by the media that entertains them. And with a lack of interaction from less playing out and more staying in to venture the World Wide Web, the prospects are somewhat harrowing. Unfortunately, this is the new norm in many homes across the western hemisphere, never mind our own nation.

"Many may be losing the art of conversation."

I do not want to get onto my soapbox or anything like that but I have worked with young people for a number of years and I have noticed that there is definitely a change of how they communicate or engage and with most of communication at home to friends and peers being via social media and the playing of games consoles there is an increase in non interpersonal communication and a lack of interface so many may be losing the art of conversation. This will cause a problem within schools and other places because as children are demanded to have good social and interpersonal skills as society requires, yet they would have lacked the practice. So when it comes to reading body language, inflection and facial expressions they will not be as able as they possibly could be. I recall a conversation with a Senior Leader within a school that I have delivered work in and what they said was a bit concerning. What they said was "I believe that there will be a generation that will have lost those vital interpersonal, life and social skills". This will cause unbalance when it comes to interaction with other generations who WOULD have such skills. This generation are dependent on social media i.e. Facebook to facilitate friendships and this has now become a norm. So when young people enter organisations where those skills are a necessity, there will be a disparity that could become detrimental to both parties but more the young people who are still on the journey of progressing in the work place and discovering these life truths.

> "This generation are dependent on social media."

Good Citizens

I remember when the term "producing good citizens" was attached with school. So the view was more holistic and not as GCSE grades driven as things seem now. More and more I am realizing; life rotates around relationships and the use of people skills. This makes people skills highly desirable and somewhat crucial, especially for young people. Speaking to another Assistant Head teacher who somewhat shared the same view and was making reference to the fact that job security is not like what it used to be, so by the time a young person is at the tender age of 30, they could have already had at least 10 jobs! So what we came to agree is, what would be highly valuable for young people to attain as well as grades is the transferable skills that could be used in a variety of industries, personal resilience as well as exceptional life and people skills. And this is why I believe it is important for young people to gain experience in a more holistic sense of education that would include both the formal and informal aspects. If this was applied, it would help many to progress in life via whatever pathway they choose.

Fact: To be mentored by a professional in the same field you desire to work within will give you an edge over someone who is not. This would also look better on your CV as you are being exposed to further professional development.

What does loco parentis mean?

When a child leaves the care of their parent and comes to school, the parent then passes over the right to the school to act on the parent's behalf with their child. And the right is not passed back to the parent until the school gets permission via a call or the child goes out of the school gate (at the right time). Now I think that this is crucial because linking it back to the rounded sense of education, I believe a school has the obligation and even the moral duty of care as a loco parentis to deliver more than academics or at least provide as many opportunities as possible for broader learning. Schools have a responsibility to provide a variety of educational learning experiences that will equip young people for life as well as a readiness to complete their academic grades. This can be in the shape of personal and social educational, vocational studies as well as life, social and personal skills as these are very crucial for success. I know that this was more emphasized when I was at school and I heard the good citizens' term more often. But, I feel that as educators nowadays, it is more about pushing everyone regardless of their shape through a square peg and doing whatever it takes to make sure they get their 5 A*- C GCSE grades. This statement was confirmed by two Head teachers who echoed the same sentiment. One shared that school is like a result factory whilst the other shared it was a factory for exams. But going back to what I said earlier "you cannot give what you do not have" so where will children pick up these soft skills i.e. relational, social and people skills? If they do not have a significant exposure to healthy opportunities where they can be formed? With a lack of interface, growing classroom sizes, greater emphasis on academic studies and to the out routing of vocational studies and other pressures such as the dreaded budget cuts, the road is not looking too hopeful at present.

You need to develop people skills

My view may seem a bit cynical but, I am still optimistic that things can improve or at least in some organizations they are doing the right thing. However, my realist views are fuelled by the multitude of examples I have experienced that I am now sharing with you. From delivering a countless amount of mentoring sessions with young people and speaking to adults (both teachers and parents) I have discovered many have the same concerns. I see education as a tool to equip young people in preparation for life and in many instances I do not feel the formality and lack of diversification of the curriculum now is truly doing so. I meet a lot of students who attend school and desire to learn, but are not ready to learn because of the other competencies they need to learn first such as social skills or listening skills. Is it just me or is there a common assumption that pupils must know how to listen but the matter of fact is many adults have not learnt how to listen effectively and are still in the process of learning; such as myself. There is a difference between listening and actively listening, which I discovered from counseling lessons.

 Top tips for mentors when listening

1. Focus on what the mentee is saying and be aware of what they are not saying.

2. Do not judge the mentee based on past experiences.

3. Do not fill the silences as you can change the direction of the conversation.

4. Await the right time to speak and avoid the temptation of rushing the mentee.

5. Do not assume, ask if you need clarity.

During my counselling studies they spoke on the discipline of actively listening where you would not be thinking of the next thing to say or what you're going to be doing after or what you are going to have for lunch etc. but you are to engage by listening attentively to what is being said and being empty of your own thoughts to be able to do so. This level of listening is very necessary especially if you have to listen to teachers or lecturers within lessons, but it is not something that is taught but expected. I guess you can call it the hidden curriculum but something so vital should not be hidden.

Case Study:
Parent's Perspective

CS

Firstly I would like to give God thanks for the mercies that he has shown me and one of the mercies is you, Herman.

As a mother my son meant the world to me and still does. I love him with a love that I believe is perfect but I also know that his walk over a two year period was quite tough for him. While he was at school he was bought up in church and came from a loving home, however as the years went on his father and I separated and within a month of separating I started to see a change in my son.

He was still amazing and loving, however he developed a small amount of anger and I was unable to pin point where it was coming from. Even though his father lived away from the house I was there and would tell him and my daughter every day how much I loved and adored them. I also enrolled them both in every activity going making sure I was there supporting them and was also very strict on their education.

On a few occasions I had to call my brother in law because Ren always wanted to go out. What I did not know was he turned to his friends for comfort and believed that's where he belonged which was very confusing for him.

I bought him a mobile phone so that I would know where he was at any given time; however I was worried a lot of the time because as a mother you want to know your child is ok.

One day Ren came home and told me he had a mentor, but I did not understand what for and why. I then met this mentor who was Herman and my heart automatically just clicked; his love for my son was just amazing, he re-instilled and opened up the passion that Ren already had in him to do well. Things then started to change at home: Ren started drum lessons and got an A* in music in one year. He then went on to get his 10 A-C GCSEs, 4 A levels and a Degree in Music and Media.

When I look back and see the angel that God sent my son who himself believed in God I am truly overwhelmed to what my son has been through and has come out the other end.

My advice to every child and to every mother and father is if your child needs help speak to the child and to the school and get them help. Sometimes as parents we take it up on ourselves to make decisions but never consider how the children would cope with separation; we need to think first then act. I am one of the mothers that have lived it and have succeeded with a beautiful son who now looks after children like himself, giving back what was given to him. My answer is trust in God because if you do that He will guide, protect and look after you.

*Herman, thank you for everything you have done for me you,
succeeded where I failed and I am grateful for your attention to
detail. To my wonderful son, I love you with a perfect love; you are
my heart and a perfect, upstanding and wonderful human being to
me.*

Love always,
Ms D Johnson

Spending time together

Remember the gangster movies where you had some baddies
who had a racket and strongly insisted on you paying
protection money or you ended up in a walk in freezer hung
up next to Peppa Pig? No not really (my little girls would not
be impressed if they heard me). Anyway, in those gangster
movies where they wore the best threads and drove the best
cars and owned the best property and were totally ruthless
concerning business or betrayal, there is something that still
stands out for me. Do you recall the scene where they were
all gathered together around the dinner table and discussed
family matters and how everyone was and who was dating
whom and so forth? This aspect of everyday life in western
society has become less important and somewhat extinct.
A lack of family interaction - and I know there is a wide
variety of families now: two parent families, single parent
families, children in foster care without their natural family
etc. however the word family is still attached to all types of
family but - are families bonding as family or simply being
familiar and taking each other for granted? Are children now
eating around a table with their parents, parent or carer?
Are they talking about things? Developing those life skills?
Are they having debates and learning how to share their
views in an articulate way? I'm afraid not as much as they
used to if at all! And definitely not as much as some of those

families in the gangster movies, where this scene was a ritual, an everyday occurrence and I would go as far as saying an event. Many children spend more time sitting in front of their TV with Daddy PS3 and Mommy Nintendo Wii and are consumed by false reality for hours on end, without much family interaction at all. I think these can be the cheapest and yet most costly babysitters around as we lose out on precious time to bond and develop those key soft skills that we get from talking, interacting, reading body language, listening to words funnelled through inflection to experience what communication is really about. And this deficit has great consequences when the children go to school.

Children having children

What is also very common place is young parents (and they are getting younger) which can cause their own problems. The reason being, children are still growing and discovering who they are and what part they are to play in society etc. So by having a child early in that process, by bringing another life into the world, the parent (who is still a child) their individual development can be somewhat stunted or put on pause to some extent as they centre their learning around how to become a parent and care for their child. The process may not be that black and white, but having children encourages you to not be so self-absorbed which is a good thing but it can be at the sacrifice of one's personal maturity and development. This then can have a bearing on the child as the challenge to pass on what you are yet to attain does present itself. One of the biggest concerns that I hear as I travel from school to school is difficult or uncooperative parents and the challenges that they present a school. And funny enough this brings me back to what I shared earlier concerning the assumptions that are commonly made about children that enter the education system. It is an expectation that there should be some social norms, values, morals, skills and competencies taught by parents or imparted by parents to their children but, how do you give what you do not have? And this is a big deficiency that can be found within many communities. In my experience I have found that some parents are challenged by their lack of knowledge when it comes to helping their children progress within school and shy away from the opportunity to help as it may show the chink in their amour. School books become like kryptonite to Super parents not because they desire not to help but their personal lid is exposed when their children are bringing home work they are not able to do because they found school difficult themselves.

"School books become like kryptonite to Super parents."

As I said, all education cannot be academia focused and I whole heartedly do not believe that a person is valued because they did well in school or that they will definitely make it in life because they have a school education because it is not the case. Some of the most successful business men and women in the world did not finish their formal education but dropped out; people such as Bill Gates, Richard Branson and the late Steve Jobs of Apple. I could reel off at least 20 more high profile millionaires and billionaires that didn't have degrees to make a name and life for themselves. But in no shape or form do I frown upon education and understand that having core skills such as the command of English for communication purposes of speaking, listening and writing and maths to understand calculations concerning understanding maths for the administration of your life i.e. your change from the shop, budgeting, adding and subtracting is crucial! And if these skills are not attained it will sadly limit your prospects especially in the society that we live in and where things are going and with University fees going up there is a great chance of fewer people going down that route, or at least there will need to be greater consideration before doing so, so hopefully we will have more Richard Bransons. Take it from me, I also found English and maths a challenge when I was at school. As Donna my wife asserted on our drive from university as she is about to embark on her own journey to become a British Sign Language Interpreter; (I am so proud of her), I probably would have been more successful in school if I had a clear reason that I was passionate about that encouraged me to gain specific grades i.e. if my aspiration was academic etc. But I wanted to be a footballer so some of my studies were not relevant to me, so I lacked motivation to do well in them. So what about the students who are like me whose aspiration is non academic or they cannot see the point?

At the same time, I have learnt more concerning the use of words through writing poetry (raps & rhymes) as I would trawl through a thesaurus and rhyming dictionary to find the perfect syllabic partnerships and the most esoteric of meanings to cause my listeners to dig for the relevance. So the carrot and finding the motivation for learning as Donna shared with me is so important. I was passionate, engaged and interested To learn rapping and rhyming so this fuelled my desire to learn more about language and the use of it.

"It's all about the packaging."

What is the carrot?

This phrase was a bit odd to me when I first heard it but the more that I use it, the more it makes sense. The analogy of the carrot and the stick focuses on the bait that would be placed before a donkey to motivate the donkey to keep travelling forward. As the Donkey chased the carrot (which would never get closer) the incentive kept the donkey moving forward as long as he desired the carrot. This one jewel has revolutionised my approach towards youth engagement and achievement and it has gained me results time and time again. The secret is, once I have identified the student's desired aspiration that is the point of how to move the student forward and their aspiration becomes their own carrot. What I have observed from this approach is students become switched on and motivated to then achieve in the same environment and educational setting. Learning is not passive, so students must be willing to engage in their lessons to ensure; the information they are taught can be grasped, retained and regurgitated. So it takes energy to actively listen and focus to also retain the information absorbed. So those who truly benefit from education are those that willingly engage and can see their own carrot which helps them to persevere and overcome external and internal adversity. For some learning is easier to access and they are able to take strides forward but for others, there is more of a challenge hence an even greater need for them to identify their carrot. For this reason, I believe education at present has got it wrong and this contributes to why so many young people leave school and become NEET (Not in Employment Education Training). Many schools focus on getting students to complete their studies but with a minor emphasis on discovering what their student's talents or passions are and what they want to become or do in life. So those who do not have at least an inkling or do not get a personal epiphany on the overall benefits of engaging in education are going to find it hard to be motivated or inspired to dig deeper to get the most out of their educational experience. Sir Ken Robinson has done an excellent talk on this www.youtube.com/watch?v=zDZFcDGpL4U it is one of the reasons why a lot of children become marginalised and do not enthusiastically complete school because they lack a personal vision and reason why school achievement is imperative and important. Plus they are not connected to their passion which is so normal within formal education. It's all about the packaging.

"I don't like crusts!" this is a common cry from children that many parents have heard and I am sure are fed up of. I am from the old school that would say the crust is the best part but my daughter just was not buying it. I remember this cry from my eldest daughter Saffron who despised eating the crust of the bread, whether toasted or sandwiches she just didn't want to eat it. Then one day I had an Isaac Newtown moment.... and you could use it as well. What I did was I toasted the bread, cut off the crusts then I asked my daughter "do you want some dippers?" and I offered her some Barbeque sauce with the crusts and guess what... she ate the crusts and sauce then said it was nice! Now this really baffled me but in a good way because for years she would not eat the crusts of toast but now she ate the same crust, same bread with a little sauce. But I then realised... it is all about the packaging, presentation and carrot principle. You see my daughter wanted a nice eating experience and she perceived crusts never fit in that equation. But by shaping the BBQ sauce and dippers idea, it then fitted into what she wanted, a bit of a Jedi mind trick.

Carrots help you to see in the dark

The carrot symbolises incentive and from working with some of the most disengaged students to engage them I would have to identify their carrot. I realised that young people always have a carrot, something that drives them, something they desire; the challenge is identifying it! And something they want deep down! Now the reality is this carrot may not be academic or "obviously" connected to their educational success i.e. grades, however if they cannot identify a link or correlation between school achievement and their carrot they may not be inspired to do much. As I mentioned earlier, education cannot be viewed just as academic so how we educate students or motivate them does need to be somewhat creative. For example: I could speak to a student who says they want to become a business man and the conversation may go like this:

Me: "So you want to be a business man but, in what area of business? And what would you like to do in the business?"

Student: "Deal with paying the wages, I'm not sure what business but it will be one of my father's."

Me: "So do you like maths?"

Student: "Not really, I just like handling money."

Me: "How could you desire such an important job like taking care of wages when you do not even have an interest in maths? Playing such a role is so important and you could be messing with people's livelihood if you got your calculations wrong. Did your father work hard to have his business?"

Student: "Yes he did, he's always at work."

Me: "Do you think your father would like his business to be ruined? And if not, why should your Dad give you a lot of responsibility in this kind of role, if you're not interested in learning a good level of Maths? And not only that, should your Dad allow you to get a better job than someone who is more dedicated and has studied hard in preparation for the opportunity?

Student: "Probably not, I never looked at it like that."

Me: "Think about it, I know your Dad must want the best for you but you still must do your part."

It may seem challenging however; I have found young people to be quite endearing when you are firm and fair with them as they know you care. Tough love must be employed to gain a level playing field where your engagement is based on truth, openness, and genuine concern for their future and lives. I have found this kind of approach to be highly successful as everything is about the carrot and psychological. For this student wanting to work in a business was his carrot. For his progression he needed to work harder in his maths lessons which would help him to make his aspiration stead fast and not based on naivety and an assumption he'd land the role because he is family.

"I do not care how much you know, until I know how much you care."

For us to really create opportunities for young people and educate them holistically whilst we exercise our - in loco parentis duties we need to really mean that every child matters. Not only does every child matter it is also remembering that they will come with unique strengths and weaknesses and if we are acutely aware of these we would be more equipped and able to get the best out of them more effectively. Ultimately, this would enable students to achieve more due to the sincere care and concern for their ultimate good even if that means they will not do well via GCSE exams. I heard a saying once which has stuck with me and it goes like this "I do not care how much you know, until I know how much you care" and sometimes with schools or other educational establishments due to governmental targets and pressure to perform can so easily miss what really matters - students are people before potential grades and will always come to school with a life attached to them that is their context.

I am really for education, I believe education opens up possibilities, options and can propel us into better positions to access a wider range of opportunities, but I also know that true education is more than scholastic and not solely measured by tests, books and exams but is about the knowledge of and ability to practice self awareness. There is a balance to be attained because without an holistic sense of true education which is the knowledge of self, life, people, overcoming challenges and living through it all, many will not experience fulfilment and joy even if they were holders of diverse qualifications. On the flip side, it is a travesty when some oppress many by withholding the right for them to having an education which you can find the mindset in the following paragraph.

"In our dreams, we have limitless resources and the people yield themselves with perfect docility to our molding hands. The present education conventions fade from our minds, and unhampered by tradition, we work our own good will upon a grateful and responsive rural folk. We shall not try to make these people or any of their children into philosophers or men of learning, or men of science. We have not to raise up from among them authors, editors, poets or men of letters. We shall not search for embryo great artists, painters, musicians nor lawyers, doctors, preachers, politicians, statesmen, of whom we have an ample supply."

– Frederick Gates, 1913 Director of Charity Rockerfeller Foundation

You wouldn't believe that there are such individuals who think in such a way but there are and it shows how important education is. One of my greatest frustrations is that a lot of our young people lack the understanding of how important education is for their futures and not only formal education but the reality that learning is more than academic but essential to progress in all areas of life. If our young could find their passion for learning, things would be different.

Question: Are you aware of what the young people around you are passionate about? If not, accept this challenge. In the next few days ask 5 young people (your children included) what they are passionate about. When you get the answers, see if there is anything you can do to encourage that passion.*

*Only assist them with their passions if it is not harmful to anyone else, positive and law abiding.

School will never be the same again...

I will never forget when my mum would say... "Your school days are the best days and when you leave school you will wish you could go back!" These words haunted me for many years, as I would have dreams about school, walking in the same corridors and queuing up for lunch and even sitting down in the canteen with friends and eating my favourite school cuisine! Yes I know this may not be the norm, but this dream would repeat and did so for years, until I started working in a school again (strange but true). I guess it brought a sense of closure as I didn't finish school as everyone else did, because I played the truant on my last afternoon, which was uncharacteristic of me, but I was influenced by a friend which I have regretted.

"I do not believe anyone can be a teacher."

Here I am now a member of staff sitting on the other side of the fence. I am now representing the adults in school after being a student for years and at times a disgruntled one. As I have grown up and experienced personal change, I also believe that school has changed and will never be the same again. The school experience is now much more intense, target driven and like a conveyor belt that is more focused on churning out 5 A* to C's than whole individuals, which is a shame.

Teacher, look at me!

My heart honestly goes out to the teachers and I do not believe anyone can be a teacher. The job of a teacher in this climate of curriculum demands, deadlines, paperwork and bureaucracy is a never ending story. Marking, planning lessons and those with pastoral duties have to communicate with home and carers etc. Never mind dealing with challenging students that couldn't care less about being in school! With larger class sizes teachers are being stretched more and more, and with the need to differentiate their teaching so learning is accessible to all students which is necessary and right but, this now presents an even greater challenge for teachers to manage. With the dreaded budget cuts now in force and made manifest by teaching and support staff redundancy, so every area will feel the crunch but the demands to deliver, do not stop. Imagine this... some teachers are expected to deliver more due to staff shortages as well as their own workload. This must bring some teachers to breaking point. I am just sharing my observations as I truly appreciate the challenges that teachers have.

"Schools with poor results attract fewer students."

As Mr Gove bangs on that standards must be raised, students must achieve greater results and become more academic with less of a vocational emphasis to fill the skills gap that exists within the work market. School league table points are under national scrutiny and even worse, if you have experienced life below that dreaded 30% (now 35) A to C in English and Maths threshold, you then gain the spotlight as a National Challenge school with Central, and Local government plus Ofsted breathing down your neck. This has now been exacerbated by the threshold going up to 50% 5 A to C's by 2015 without concessions, and the atmosphere and working environment cannot be nice for the staff or pupils. But this is the new reality. Schools with poor results attract fewer students, in doing so attract less funding that comes with each student and not forgetting the National Curriculum that demands one size fits all, forcing circles through square pegs! This cannot be a healthy inclusive environment to raise well balanced children in. It is so high octane with Head teachers having to make their school happen regardless of their resources. I know of one Head who was working with a £700,000 deficit budget, in other words a humungous overdraft, so even at the start of the new financial year after receiving their new budget they were over half a million pounds short and not one new pound had been spent!

Behaviour, Behaviour, Behaviour

More and more schools and traditional set ups are finding the task of dealing with students who present behavioural challenges overwhelming, as the world from outside the school now inevitably comes in. Since times are changing and children are ever more aware of their rights, this is more challenging to accommodate, so many work hard at containing these students, which is not a good alternative as many young people are not engaged. Containment does not produce the desired fruits of responsible young people that would be able to positively contribute to society. The problem is if this is not remedied in school where attendance is mandatory, where there is the opportunity to collaboratively have a crack at the whip with parents, it may need to happen within the criminal justice system which adds greater expense and challenge to our communities.

What is needed is a new approach. How refreshing would it be for many young people if they had someone really taking the time out for them, who was appropriately skilled with multiple intelligences that suited their differentiated needs? Intelligences such as emotional, interpersonal, social and cultural would not go amiss in such a climate of misunderstanding and higher expectations for students to succeed within school and society itself. With times changing, budgets being cut, homes being affected, crime being committed, youth unemployment now peaked above one million, fewer job opportunities to access, things are not looking hopeful. But we can't stop and just throw in the towel as our needs still exist; the younger generation still need to be nurtured so they can contribute in a meaningful way.

"We need more people who are specifically trained and skilled to work with young people."

The issue many still face the young people are going to be in schools as it is still compulsory and parents have a duty to send their children or face fines and, at worst, prison sentences. So my question is... where is this all heading? In over 15 years' mentoring experience, engaging with a multitude of students and having a keen eye in the inner cities, I can say from my observations and experience of working in schools and in the inner city... If we are going to predict according to the maxim "it must get worse before it gets better" then we are in for some challenging times ahead, if we do not do something different. My question is - what is going to be done within schools, academies other organisations to engage their young people with staff who are on the brink of collapse, or worse yet, just giving up?

Regardless of resources, budgets or legislation we need more people who are specifically trained and skilled to work with young people. Because if staff are not being equipped for the storm they will have to face on the front line, why would they be placed there? It is sad to say they are being set up to fail! School, at present, is the only place that is compulsory for all children to attend, so who is going to help the traditional schools deal with the stark reality that is already biting? It is easy to write white papers or green papers or have conversations in Whitehall and make forecasts from Ivory towers that are based on theory, without having a clue of the tangible or experiential reality of the implementation from policy to practicality. This gap has to be addressed because some of these white collared policy makers haven't got the foggiest, and it is a shame because their policies could change things for the better, but when change according to lofty ideas are theoretically considered to be sound, it's those on the ground that have to experience the consequences of their half-baked 'eureka' moments.

It's not all bad though...

Watching a few episodes of Jamie's Dream School, I can bet it was an eye opening experience for those who have not had the privilege of working with children who can display challenging behaviour, who are simply misunderstood. To see a variety of celebrities taking the time out to engage those who are deemed disaffected and disengaged, it is good television and I like Jamie's heart as he means it. I know that everyone has their role and jobs to make society work, however those in government and decision makers who have such an impact on the lives of others could at least get some authentic insight before they go off on a tangent by making policies that simply are short sighted and make things worse. I would be more than willing to share my years of experience and insight with those who truly desire to change the lives of young people in this country and internationally, because ultimately it is all about the children who are our future.

Who you gonna call?

The reality is, some schools are too insular and would benefit from a variety of professionals from different backgrounds with different skill sets and experiences to bridge the gap. I believe mentors are that bridge, as any mentor who is worth their weight in gold is a highly effective mediator, communicator or interpreter. A mentor who is emotionally intelligent and socially aware can understand what is being said and what is not being said and then translate it across cultural, educational and ethnical differences. As you have different races, classes, cultures and experiences with a variety of issues, conventional schooling and systems will not always be able to deal with them effectively, hence a need for a variety of educators / mentors within the community is essential.

But it is on paper...

One thing that has changed the face of school is new legislation and the school's duty to deliver various policies to ensure quality, competence and fairness. When I think about how crucial policy is, what comes to mind is Every Child Matters. Now reflecting on how it came about is very sad and unfortunate, but young Victoria Climbie (2nd Nov 1991 – 25th Feb 2000) would never know the level of impact and change her devastating demise has brought to pass. For those who are not aware, Victoria Climbie was a young girl who was neglected, starved and abused at the hand of her carers who were relatives. But what was shocking was that all the services involved i.e. the social services, her GP or educators never rang the alarm early enough to effectively intervene before she was killed. Because of this tragedy, the Every Child Matters policy was birthed for us who work with young people more holistically. Every Child Matters has clearly changed the face of children's services, how they are delivered, audited and quality assured. The same has been done by the Healthy Schools, Community Cohesion and Cultural Diversity policies, but I do not take for granted or assume that all schools are successfully, doing what they ought.

I remember whilst delivering keynote speeches for the Specialist Schools and Academies Trust (SSAT) one of my signature presentations would ask the question: "Does every child REALLY matter?" And if they do, do the children feel the same? Do the systems in your organisation and procedures confirm this claim? It is a very provoking and searching question, but the reality of it is, it is a valid point and a necessary question to ask. Also, with policy on children being excluded from school to lower the permanent exclusion rates as well as encouraging our gifted and talented students to achieve their best instead of coasting and achieving the baseline C GCSE grade, there are a lot of new legislations to ensure equity and equality in schools.

"C and above, C and above, C and above."

Even though there is a lot of legislation to safeguard and create a better environment for schools, these will also present their own challenges. If these policies are to be delivered effectively they must be more than rhetoric, but an ethos that becomes embedded within school culture and not just a bolt on. But if new legislation is delivered to benefit the children and the learning community then it is worthwhile.

The relentless pursuit of C and above grades

Just like the title 'Location, Location, Location' emphasises, the importance of the postcode of where you will buy your property is paramount. Over the last few years, in the school world it has been "C and above, C and above, C and above". This focus has been one of the most destructive tools to marginalise some students, because not all will attain this governmental benchmark due to their ability, learning style, lack of ability to perform in final exams or their talent not being academic. I know performance is important and how it enables students to access further education and work opportunities, but I have seen the culture of achievement and the need for school success increased in manifold ways to the detriment of the holistic development of well rounded individuals. If we are to be brutally honest, children who have no chance of achieving 5 C's and above are less favoured than those who will. I have seen it and heard this played out in a variety of schools, and I have seen the interventions that are put into place year in year out, especially during year 11 which is school bread and butter time. Even if we were to look at the focus of predominantly targeting those who are on the C/D borderline and making more interventions, catch up classes, mentoring, coaching, revision, additional weekend classes etc., would you say the same interventions and opportunities are accessible for students who are only ever going to get an E/F grade? I rest my case. Please understand my thinking, I get the reasoning behind why things are done in this way and it concerns school league table points, school standing and pupil achievement, but if every child matters like the policy states then there would be a balanced emphasis for all children regardless of their ability to achieve their personal best, and the resources and interventions should be readily available for all. As the title states, every child needs a mentor.

Breaking point!

The push for 5 C's and above has placed a considerable amount of pressure on schools, students, teachers and parents to achieve. This can definitely be a bit too much and is for many. Much of the pressure that students go through without a mentor to reassure and support them impacts on their well-being and is a great reason why every child needs a mentor. Many students are affected by mental health issues such as anxiety, worry, depression and panic attacks during exams season, which would be lessened if they had a significant adult to speak to besides their parents during these times. If you ask most students what have been the most stressful times in their entire school lives, over 90% will point to either year 10 or 11, which is the GCSE C and above zone. With a greater emphasis on which schools are the best to develop students in and the school league table points (which is like a premiership for schools) those schools who are more successful are able to attract better students (supposedly) and in doing so, are able to strive for and continue to attain the success they have previously experienced. For schools who do not do well, they either have Local Authority intervention or Central Government attention (some schools in 2008 who achieved under 30% 5 C's and above in English and Maths were placed on the National Challenge register in view of all to see). So I understand the pressure, but this is another reason for such a shift in the world of schooling and the educational experience of young people who need to deliver the goods when the majority lack any additional mentoring support.

What about the students?

I have engaged numerous young people from schools, universities, sixth forms, colleges, correctional facilities, on the streets, in faith groups and social events. I have done this via speaking, delivering and coordinating mentoring programmes, motivational sessions, one to one's etc. and the pressure of life and school that students are exposed to because of this new regime of raising standards and achievement really does affect some in a bad way. With an increase of anxiety, worry and insecurity of not living up to the expectations of teachers, their school, parents (who sometimes expect beyond their children's true capabilities) as well as older siblings, with whom many are compared to, this has a psychological and emotional impact on them. No wonder many students just disengage, especially when they do not have a mentor to keep them on track or encourage them personally during the low times, as they do come. Whether we want to admit it or not, a lot of young people are experiencing mental health issues because of the intense school environment and the now essential needs to succeed academically. This includes those who are not naturally academic who experience greater pressure as the curriculum is harder to access. These students rarely benefit as much as their academically inclined counterparts; so they will struggle through school.

http://www.telegraph.co.uk/education/educationnews/8720513/GCSEs-Pressure-of-exams-leaves-teens-suffering-from-mental-illness.html

There are multiple intelligences

Due to learning about various learning styles as well as reading some of the work by Howard Gardener and Tony Buzan, I truly feel that how the education system is set up is missing a trick here. A lot of people are intelligent in other ways besides the typical scholastic type that is measured via alpha and numeric methods. In schools, many students are not being identified as intelligent or being told that they are or supported appropriately and this significantly impacts their self esteem and progress, as some will feel less significant because they are not bright when tested via the National Curriculum lens.

"Which was shocking to hear."

I will never forget when I attended an emotional intelligence workshop in 2001 delivered by Dr Roy Paget, who is a Neuroscientist and leading authority on brain based learning. He specialises in educational and academic achievement of children. I remember when he spoke candidly about our National Curriculum being about 50 years behind where it should be, which was shocking to hear! It was even more alarming to hear a statement of that nature said with such authority and conviction. The reasons he gave were: children learn in a variety of ways but teaching in schools is designed to predominantly facilitate learning in two ways, auditory and visually. If you think about it, most teaching is done via oral delivery (auditory) with work being written on the board (visually) and with children being expected to sit down for long periods of time to access this learning. For many, this is a nightmare because children who are naturally kinaesthetic (movement) learners would feel awkward and it would be an unnatural way to learn.

One of my earliest educational memories was when I was in my infants school and my teacher Ms Brackley said to me "You keep fidgeting like you have ants in your pants". I can't remember what I was up to, but I knew it had negative connotations when she said it and how she said it. Could it be that I was a person that learnt better being able to move? Or was I naughty because I found it difficult to stay in my seat so that the teacher could teach me and the others in the class how it suited her? I'm not sure, but some children would naturally thrive in an academic environment whose preferred learning style borrowed itself to that type of delivery, which is most common within education. So with intelligence being mostly measured via numerical, alphabetical and spatial means, a lot of students would have an advantage, due to their natural aptitude for this teaching methodology. We are really talking about an education reform, and while that is not what I am currently focusing on, clearly education is not as "inclusive" as it claims to be.

I remember attending a training session by the world renowned Barbara Prashnig, who is a leading figure concerning learning styles. During her session she said a lot of profound things but one that has stuck with me the most is this: "Many teachers teach according to how they learn best". This statement really blew me away because she made us aware that everyone learns differently. It is hard to facilitate such personalised learning in a group scenario, which is why the power of a child having a mentor and someone who focuses on their individual progress is so powerful. With a greater awareness of learning styles, personalised learning and other considerations, schools will never be the same.

To find out more about multiple intelligences please visit: http://www.multipleintelligencetheory.co.uk/index.aspx

To see an interview by Barbara Prashnig please watch: http://www.youtube.com/watch?v=WoVPVgw9nCE

Over my knee!

I remember when I literally experienced this saying, and it was to my bottom's detriment: ouch! I'll never forget, I arrived at a new primary school, and with the new school came learning all about the new rules, expectations and boundaries. However, there were some things at this new school that I was not accustomed to and I was about to find out. I cannot remember what the misdemeanour was, but I do remember the consequences of it. I was in trouble and I was brought in front of the whole class, my Head Teacher then got me over his knee and smacked me on the bum with his white plimsoll! The shock of it... and to add insult to injury, I was entertainment or an example for the rest of the class to observe. One thing I learnt very quickly was to stay in line and not repeat that misdemeanour. I can see the funny side now, even though it is still slightly unnerving (just the thought) but effective and a definite deterrent which was clear and worked as I never got the plimsoll again. I know many of you have your own stories of being reprimanded by your head or another teacher, whether in this country or abroad, as this was previously accepted practice within schools. This episode causes me to now reflect on the state of play concerning disciplines in school. I am not an advocate for bringing the cane back, but maybe a more clear understanding of consistent action and consequence for all would be beneficial as one thing I know - children appreciate and prefer boundaries.

"1000 pupils are excluded everyday within the UK!"

Insight: "Did you know that students do not prefer teachers that they can walk all over? From the feedback students have given they prefer teachers who are emotionally consistent plus firm, friendly and fair. I call this the 3 F's approach"

I have found that the deterioration of behaviour in schools has significantly increased. In July 2011 the Department for Education (DfE) published that 1000 pupils are excluded everyday within the UK! This was predominantly for behavioural reasons, acts of violence towards teachers and general disrespect to teaching staff and their peers. It was reported that at that time, many teachers felt threatened and many have or desire to leave the profession. For this reason the government have changed some guidelines to usher the balance of power back into the hands of the teachers who under the last regime somewhat felt disempowered in their classrooms. Is there a rise in behaviour issues because there is an increase in the lack of respect for authority in general, and in schools - namely towards teachers? The relationship of the teacher and pupil is still a highly valuable asset but sadly, it is turbulent in many schools. However, the disrespect or lack of appreciation is not only found coming from the students but also from teachers.

I don't have to respect you!

I have heard of teachers saying that they don't need to respect students, but the students need to respect them. I believe the respect may be different but advisably a two way thing, and if this is commonplace it could be one of the reasons why some experience "unacceptable" defiance and rebellion from young people. I was speaking with a very senior and highly respected Deputy Head teacher named Mr Sukhbir Farah. For some time he was a line manager of mine and he is very endearing, with a generous smile and sense of humour, but in school, if students got on his bad side he has a stare that could scare the stripes off zebras! His demeanour demands respect but at the same time he is firm but fair and has a wonderful laugh and a great sense of humour. He came from a similar background to mine: a lover of sports - cricket to be exact - and grew up in the inner city, so understands the codes of the streets. What was funny about Sukhbir is I knew he had an edge but I found out little by little about his background over time. In other words, he is a dark horse but in a good way. Anyway, one day we were having a conversation about the teacher pupil relationship and respect, and as a man full of wisdom, he shared: "Teachers are misguided if they think respect is not a two way thing. Respect is not a given, it is earned! And when it is earned, the pupils will do almost anything for the teacher who has earned it". I totally agree with Mr Farah who is a teacher I highly respect. He has truly earned it. Even though I share this point, I do understand the train of thought which some adults in an authoritarian role can adopt, because even as a youngster I was told by my parents to respect my elders. However, I totally disagree with this belief that some hold, concerning the fact that respect should be given *just* because of their role and do not believe it is a two way thing. This approach may work in the army where such a level of subordination and reverence to your superior is expected, but this would be disturbing if it were a mentality that was the norm in schools. Young people are very serious about respect and if one is culturally or socially literate with an understanding, they will know respect is a very important thing, and sadly, many lose their lives because of a misguided notion of respect and disrespect in life.

"Young people are very serious about respect."

Reflection: Would you say that you are respectful towards young people? If so, would your children, relatives, students or service users say the same about you?

By no stretch of the imagination do I vouch for pupils disrespecting teachers, adults, peers or parents because I have always been the first to challenge young people who have sought my counsel, concerning issues where they have contributed to disrespecting others. What I am saying is, from experience, I have found misunderstandings between teachers and students to be common and becoming even more prevalent and is the thorn in the side of many schools, or the reason for many fixed term or permanent exclusions because of this respect and lack of respect subject. This is definitely compounded by the fact that because of the intensity of life outside the school gates i.e., the economy, community challenges, family breakdown etc. and with many teachers struggling with workloads, work-life balance and some having to take time off because of stress, it is definitely a cause for concern as unhealthy and dysfunctional relationships are on the increase and a contributing factor.

It's not fair!

One of the major problems is a disparity and a lack of consistency when it comes to dealing with behaviour. Simply, sometimes the consequences for behaviour are based upon the judgement of who executes the punishment, the pupil involved or which teacher the offence happened to (if one was involved) which is too discretionary. At times, sad to say on many occasions, it will also depend on the ethnicity of the pupil at hand, which will contribute towards how severe the punishment is - how shocking! In this day and age there is still discrimination and it is known that there is a disproportionate representation of young black boys and other ethnic minorities experiencing institutionalised racism, which has resulted in harsher punishments.

"The 3 to 1 ratio is very disproportionate."

In his report commissioned by the Department for Education and Schools (DfES, 2006), "Getting it Right" http://www.dorsetrec.org.uk/Pubs/Reports/Docs/ PriorityReviewSept06.pdf Martin Bull delivered an expose of the state of the education system when it came to punitive measures geared towards black boys. This was startling and in many circles brushed under the rug because it made for embarrassing reading. Especially in a democratic country that supposedly believes in equal opportunities and equity. In the DfES report, it stated that black boys were 3 to 1 times more likely to experience the most severe level of punishment and be permanently excluded from school than their white counterpart. The most disturbing thing was that this was based on facts and not conjectures. With black boys making such a small minority in education, the 3 to 1 ratio is very disproportionate. Even though this is quite a meaty and somewhat controversial topic with a lot to be discussed, I do not desire to delve further at this point. However, I find it necessary to just highlight the correlation between behaviour and punishment within many schools where some feel that there is a lack of fairness or organisational consistency. This can also feed into a lack of relationship and respect for the establishment which can be represented from the students and their parents.

Activity: Could you grab a piece of paper, take a moment and reflect on what you have personally found unfair in the education system? When you have written it down think about how you overcame these aspects and what has been the positive effect of combating the injustice?

You're not teaching me right!

Now to something a little lighter, as we are now living in the information age, knowledge is not limited to the methods of old, with teachers being the exclusive fonts of knowledge but now with more knowledge and information coming from the Internet, new research and social media etc. young people are more exposed to information, and some think adamantly that they know all they need to know. This is a phrase that I have heard on a number of occasions: "The teacher cannot teach" or "They are not teaching me in my learning style" or the most common one is "We're just given a book to copy out of". Truthful or not, you can never just take everything at face value. However, this new awareness of knowledge is causing many students to become overly knowledgeable in how they can avoid being engaged and getting the best out of their learning experiences. I would go as far to say that some students have become like the girl who starred in Charlie and the Chocolate Factory who was spoilt and had to have her own way until her own way led to her own demise.

One of our challenges now as a society is that we have fought for every right, so everyone has the right to be right, so who is going to be wrong if everyone is right? Children now know their rights, many times to their own detriment. I have seen this on many occasions: instead of children being smart in a way that benefits their progress, they are smart in a way that hinders them from being all that they could be. I have observed when a pupil cries wolf stating that they have been inappropriately handled by a member of staff, so the staff member is then under suspicion. Then to have the truth come out and the student found to be conniving, untrue and their allegation fabricated.

Rights, rights, rights! Our society has gone crazy and this is totally another discussion which I do not wish to engage in, especially with those who have a nonsensical view of how you should implement these rights. For instance, who remembers the whole health and safety argument where in some schools, students have to wear safety goggles and a hard hat to play conkers?! Policy has gone too far! I know we need guidelines. We need to be aware that if policies are not administered sensibly, then many can fall victim to these guidelines that then become harmful to common courtesy and sense.

All in all, the entire school world has changed and there is no going back. But being aware of the changes and some of the things that could be done to address the balance would make the experience better for all involved.

Activity – School will never be the same again

1. In reflection, what did you enjoy the most when you were at school?

2. What 2 things could you have done to have made your school experience even better?

3. During your school years who was a mentor for you?

4. What would you radically change about school if you could?

5. Knowing what you know and given the current situation in our society - What would be your best bit of advice to young people concerning education?

The Hope for Mentoring

RAMP® - Raising Achievement Mentoring Programmes

I'll never forget, in 2005 as a part of a hostile takeover, which in education terms is called a Hard Federation, I was part of a consultancy team that was on an assignment to help turn around a failing school whose Head Teacher was removed and my boss at the time had now assumed the role of the Executive Head teacher.

My role on this project was to engage some of the students who were bright but were disenfranchised with the whole school experience. During this time, I developed a few interventions that focussed on helping the students to improve their conduct within school, realise their potential and to understand the importance of completing their school career. Whilst helping them to be inspired, I was also inspired as I created a mentoring approach called RAMP® - Raising Achievement Mentoring Programmes. The whole idea behind the philosophy was to help students to elevate above their circumstances and obstacles so they could achieve higher attitudes and altitudes. So that was it, I called it RAMP and the strap line I created was "Helping others to elevate their attainment".

LoL!

One day, I remember sharing this concept to my then line manager Ms Emson who just laughed out loud, and after laughing her head off, repeating the word 'ramp'! I could have easily been offended because I was dead serious but, Kate and I had such a great working relationship and she was such a supporter of my work, and because of her years of pastoral knowledge and experience wielded great influence within the school. On top of all that, she was a ex teacher of mine from my secondary school St John Wall, so we had known each other for a long time. I understood her and no offense was taken. I am glad that I kept the name RAMP because it has not only changed my view of mentoring but has also changed the view of many educators, as well as the lives of countless young people.

As I wrote earlier in the book, within education mentoring has been viewed by many as a behaviour management strategy however, mentoring was now about to be used in an all encompassing way.

"Can't see the wood from the trees."

Who should be mentored?

Mentoring is about empowerment, motivation and enablement to help the mentee achieve their personal potential. This may sound straight forward and is where the challenge comes in as the saying goes 'can't see the wood from the trees' hence the need from an external perspective and this is the benefit of a mentor. It can be difficult to be objective when it comes to your own personal development, but the RAMP strategy is to put the child in the centre of a positive mentoring community that connects students, staff, parents and the wider and business or sports community. So the mentee experiences a holistic support mechanism that is undergirded with aspirant and positive language which encourages the desired results.

Aspiring can be tiring...

I remember when I first came across the word "aspiration". I remembered inspiration but aspiration was different and a word I should have been acquainted with. You see, aspiration was the very word that encapsulated my life and its approach, it was what I had been doing for many years as I aspired to be a football player, a successful professional recording artist and successful in mentoring. I consistently strived to go beyond my current circumstances to be more than what I was, to achieve what I had never achieved before, which embodied aspiration. Now through RAMP my mission is to help a generation of young people to identify their carrot by acknowledging what their personal strengths and aspirations are and helping them to develop a passion, focus and discipline to achieve it! The RAMP mentoring model is about helping mentees to increase their personal effectiveness, believe in their own ability so they can experience personal fulfilment in their school, home and relationships. This is achieved by making young people aware of their possibilities regardless of where they are starting from, as well as taking on board responsibility for their actions, thoughts, attitudes and beliefs. All of this is to empower young people with the reality that they can learn from both their successes and failures as they develop personal accountability and resilience, and the power of understanding positive and negative consequences can both be beneficial to their development.

Failure is not final

I remember when my pastor once said to me that "failure is not final" which has stuck with me. The big thing about the RAMP ethos is it is totally inclusive, so any individual could enter this process regardless of their level of success as it is about getting the best out of the mentee, and not simply just helping a mentee to behave better. The RAMP process is not based on a deficit model, it is preventative, proactive and an assertive model that is also reactive to accommodate crisis management. For this reason, I believe that every child needs a mentor as RAMP Mentoring encompasses the whole spectrum, so all students who need some form of support during their school career have equal access to the provision. I also believe RAMP Mentoring should be started from primary school so the transition from year 6 to year 7 in secondary school is not so steep and they get a great chance to acclimatise.

You may ask what is difference between RAMP mentoring and other mentoring? Well, in a nut shell, RAMP is a preventative and aspirant mentoring process that is truly inclusive in its approach and is implemented strategically with a framework that enables mentoring to be delivered in a more robust, coherent and effective way. RAMP Mentoring provides informal learning opportunities by providing nourishing support and positive challenges for the whole teaching and learning community, not just a select few. The RAMP model was developed with the ability to facilitate the essential learning and supportive conversations that would need to take place as well as being qualitative and quantifiable by design to ensure quality and credibility.

Below you can see the difference between the commonly used model within education and the RAMP model:

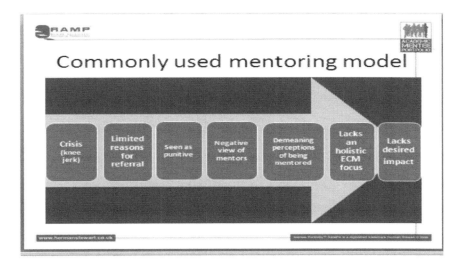

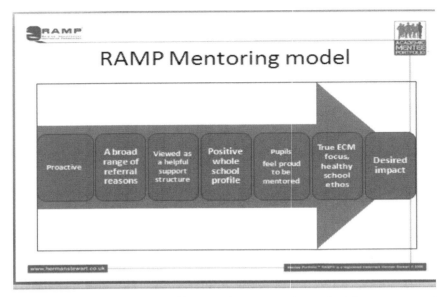

The models above display the difference in preventative and crisis management mentoring approaches. The commonly used mentoring model shows a lack of inclusion, is prone to be viewed negatively and promotes the deficit model approach while the RAMP model is proactive, encourages inclusivity and student achievement.

There are many ways to skin a cat

If Donna heard me say this, or any of my 3 daughters, they would probably gang up on me because we have got a pet cat called "Smokey", but all can rest assured no cats were harmed in the writing of this book and I am figuratively speaking. Just as there are many ways to skin a cat there are many ways to engage, inspire and motivate young people (and older ones too). For this matter, I created various mentoring programmes to provide students with a range of supportive pathways for their development. To create an all inclusive mentoring strategy you would need access to a diversity of mentors with varying backgrounds, skills, experience and levels of expertise. This would be of paramount importance. Every child does matter so every child should be able to grow accordingly by the support that we provide. Below I have listed a number of mentoring programmes that we delivered:

The Community model: Where I would have trained mentors from the community who had an altruistic desire to give something back. This mentor may not be highly skilled with a broad spectrum of techniques for the diversity of needs that mentoring can address. So these mentors would be supported by more experienced mentors but they would still add value.

The College model: These mentors would come and deliver a mentoring programme fitting to their brief. As the mentors would be from college, and volunteering to get their experience to pass their course, they would only have access to a very specific brief of student.

The CSR model: This would be delivered by personnel from the private sector who desired to give something back, and at the same time satisfying their companies' Corporate, Social Responsibility (CSR) aspirations. These mentors would be highly skilled in a variety of disciplines so the mentors could be chosen strategically and paired up appropriately for maximum effect.

The Transition model: This approach would focus on the two transitions that are critical within the school environment (many schools miss out the most "important"transition which is neither year 6 to 7 or 11 to 12). This programme would focus on those who are making the transition to ensure the process is as seamless as possible.

The Academic model: Which would focus on enabling a number of different staff from senior leaders, teachers, TA's and form tutors to deliver a more academically focussed coaching model to a designated number of students to raise their attainment.

The last but most important mentoring aspect, which is:

The Pastoral model: This would deliver an in house service to children in need of support for issues such as: parental separation, self harming, bullying, bereavement, looked after children who needed additional support, gang affiliates, those with challenging behavior and low self-esteem just to name a few. These mentors would be highly skilled in people skills as well as cultural, emotional and interpersonal intelligence with a great understanding of how to mediate between diverse communities. They would also require exemplary people skills as they would have to address a variety of complex issues.

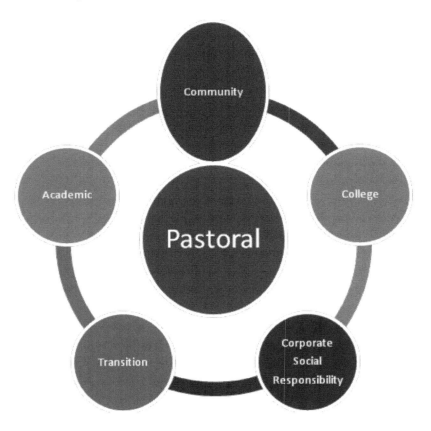

Above see the RAMP Mentoring model with its heart being the pastoral care component

Now the secret to having all of the above working succinctly and cohesively is the innovative RAMP framework. Without the components for the programme all of the above would fall on its face or spin out of control and create more organisational issues than solutions. For this reason the structural foundation and personnel to operate it is crucial.

The RAMP model has been created to support young people who are experiencing a variety of skill gaps whether they are educational or personal. By providing this level of support for mentees, we had successfully opened up the perception of mentoring and its effectiveness. Also, many young people who once would not have even been considered for mentoring were now accessing the vital support. Children could now be mentored from all backgrounds with all issues, presenting diverse needs and varying levels of concern. The RAMP strategy is also a great NEET remedy as it focuses on students from a pre-NEET stage enabling students to have much more road before them so they can truly fly when they get to the end of the year 11 runway. I am truly convinced and a firm believer that to prevent NEETs you must start the process as early as year 4 and as late as year 9! Even though with great effort and resources you could do emergency work in year 10 and 11. The RAMP philosophy is this, catch children while they are still dreaming and nurture the possibility of the dream and ground it with the components and support necessary for it to happen!

Pupil Voice

Below are the responses from a variety of students who have had the RAMP experience.

"My attitude has been more positive towards school."

"My school work has improved and my grades. It has made me feel more motivated to complete my work."

"It's made me more independent and I realise what I have to do to reach my goals."

"Has given me the confidence to move forward."

"It means a great deal to me as I would not be where I am today without this."

"It has helped me to work harder and sort out applying for colleges and I've thought a lot about what I want to do when I leave school."

"A new chance... a new beginning."

"It has helped me realise I have potential. I don't have to follow others and do nothing."

"Increased my work process and I am not that lazy anymore."

"I am always good in lessons and get on with my work now. Before I used to talk."

"The layout of my writing has changed and my results have improved."

"The whole experience has been very enlightening"

"I have found all the sessions fun and inspiring and have helped me to do things in a different way"

"Yes, I have become more focused on my work and I think I am a better person""It was really exciting just to be real about myself and I feel proud of who I am"

"I've stopped messing about in lessons"

"It's changed my life, I used to mess about and not care about school but now I do"

"Very inspiring and has made me think about the future and has made me work harder in class"

"My attitude towards learning has changed for the better"

"I have realized that education is a lot more important than I thought"

Fact:
Did you know that a school year is only 190 days!

It's never too late!

In some school circles it is deemed as too late to engage those in year 11 to make significant gains due to most of the progress or damage already having been done, and their predicted grades having been calculated. However, it is never too late to stop someone from becoming a NEET statistic and it is never too late to inspire someone! As a part of the RAMP city wide programme that we rolled out in Birmingham, we witnessed all schools that delivered RAMP experienced either improvements in their grades, punctuality, attendance, behaviour or student engagement and the students also testified of their own attitudinal shifts and eureka moments (later in the book you can read the case study). For this work I received a Leading Aspect Award for narrowing the gap in achievement and raising the morale, well-being, performance and attainment of year 10 and 11 students. So it is never too late to turn the corner given you employ the right strategies, tools and philosophies. And it is so important to find out what the students need instead of what you "think" they need.

Can you mentor me?

Historically and even at present many schools still focus on two sections of pupils and pour much needed resources into these groups. The first group is the underachievers and the second group is the gifted and talented, who will do well, but how well is the concern. These groups can be seen as the top and the bottom groups and in both groups, but probably more in the bottom one, there are students who present behavioural problems within the school. Now due to both of these groups receiving a lot of attention from the school the middle group of students who are sometimes termed as the invisibles are overlooked which is where most of the schools wealth and potential lies. This is not my theory but is also recognised by John Hill who is a Researcher and very familiar with statistics within the Birmingham LA as well as other analytical professionals.

To gain more understanding concerning the invisibles you can read this section from a Google book where they are spoken about: http://bit.ly/wAnZlU

Student targeting happens from data collection and then the appropriate interventions are put in place to curb underachievement or maximise high achievement, as these are considered somewhat 'in the bag'. At the same time schools do strive to get the best out of those in the middle with the greatest emphasis placed on those who are C/D borderline, so some are targeted as well but many are not.

To a great extent I do understand why things are done this

way, it is because those who are disruptive create lots of situations that need to be addressed hence the financial investment for support or external provision if necessary. Due to this approach many children who are not viewed as priority are not treated urgently but left to their own devices. Sadly this community of young people suffer silently and are at the cusp of becoming one of those who will need greater attention because they are not flagged up earlier as a concern. This is where the RAMP mentoring model is most relevant and effective. The RAMP process focuses on the whole child, so it has the ability to identify issues earlier. This enables you to address 'most' issues proactively and where possible; they can be nipped in the bud.

I am amazed...

I am always amazed at the attempts made to divorce academic achievement from pastoral care. If you are able to do this you are also able to separate a child's scholastic ability from their personal, social and emotional needs which is impossible. So children need to be viewed in a holistic way if we are to truly get the best out of them. For this reason, I view children as adults that are yet to be fully grown but have the same needs such as respect, acceptance, patience, validation, praise and consideration. I recognise the issues many young people have such as low self-esteem, lack of identity or not wanting to embrace their differences because it's easier to blend in the crowd. I have experienced similar challenges, so mentoring has to be all encompassing and a truly dynamic support system that can support all things academic and beyond. But before this can happen you will need a referral process that welcomes all who desire mentoring.

How do I get a mentor?

The long and short of it is your mentoring programme will

not be as productive if it does not allow the pupils who need it the most to access it when needed. Please ask yourself the following questions:

- What types of students are on the mentoring programme?

- Does the profile of your typical mentee represent a cross section of students within your school?

- Would it be fair to say that those mentored are stereotyped by being mentored?

If your answer is the latter then you have a referral process problem. If your programme poses a form of discrimination, whether positive or negative, it could make some students worse than better in the short and long term because if they are stereotyped by being mentored it will reinforce the negative views held by some within the school community and by the mentee themselves. And if only students that are considered to be smart receive academic mentoring it can create resentment amongst students who deem it unfair. You could truly desire to help your students but the possibility of further stigmatisation due to the mentoring programme's design is highly likely, so it then ends up being a downward spiral for the student and possibly their remaining school career. For some schools when mentoring fails it actually means that the students are close to being permanently excluded – in other words – they are out! An inclusive referral process ensures that every child could access mentoring support because of the broad spectrum of reasons why they could be referred. This then ensures that all children from high, medium to underperformers who present a variety of needs between key stage 2 and 4, can enjoy additional mentoring support without the negative label that some mentoring programmes attach to their users.

Case Study –
Letter from a parent of a mentee

CS

As a parent of a child who had a mentor at secondary school, I would acknowledge how grateful I was that he came into my son's life and had a positive impact on my child.

My son was given a mentor at school when he was going through a difficult time within the educational system, because he challenged authority and pushed the boundaries. What was so hard to bear was my son was an intelligent young man who was capable of achieving his dreams and aspirations, if he set his mind to putting in some work. Instead, he was contributing the bare minimum which meant he often clashed with authority.

This resulted in frustration for me having to have a telephone conversation with his Year Head and me having to attend the school, which often made my son's behaviour worse. When your child gets labelled as a troublemaker it's hard for them to have confidence in their abilities and could result in low self-esteem.

When a mentor was suggested, I was more than willing to give this a try with my son's consent, because if he didn't want to take part there would be no point. I met the mentor and talked about my son and the problems he was experiencing. I felt confident that he had my son's best interest at heart and would provide support and guidance. He kept me regularly updated on my son's progress and I myself could see an improvement in his behaviour and his academic studies improved and his self-esteem and confidence were also boosted.

He used his experiences in a positive way to indirectly mentor his peers using his own knowledge and because they could relate to him quicker than the teachers.

He has further used these experiences and is now a mentor himself working with children who are at risk of being excluded from school and I am so proud of his achievements and I would say if he didn't have a mentor I don't think he would have decided on that career, but because of his experiences and the impact of having a mentor, he wanted to give something back and he really enjoys the challenge each child brings.

Every child deserves to have a mentor, who will make a lifelong impression in a child's life, if they are open to the challenge.

Yaminah Kondwani

Many schools are missing a trick here...

One of the greatest frustrations that I have is how many mentoring programmes are misunderstood and unsuccessfully delivered in education. If we were simply to look at mentoring as we do in business, sports, music or any of the arts, this would take only a small paradigm shift but would make a life changing difference up and down the country for students, parents, teachers and entire communities. If the value of mentoring was perceived or understood as important or its potential recognized; there would be more concerted effort into making it what it could be.

"Free support sounds great but caution is to be employed!"

From my experience mentoring works best in an organisation when it is supported by a senior leader who is a passionate advocate for children. For mentoring to be all it can it must be viewed as "whole school" and not just something that is done from September for year 11 students to get prepared for their final exams. Even though there is nothing wrong with using mentoring in this way, it just shouldn't stop there. For this programme to work effectively the senior leader would designate a key person who is given the time, authority and responsibility to provide direction for the programme's whole school implementation. If you are global in your thinking you can also source out a variety of additional support opportunities for the school to receive skilled help for free! This could be done via partnering with a local business who would like to engage with a school to increase their CSR options etc. Free support sounds great but caution is to be employed! Such programmes can present logistical challenges so one must seek professional guidance when developing such approaches. Include local colleges, universities and other organisations who could add value to your students and establishment. I am sure you can see how it could grow, hence needing more skilled personnel and this approach does not need to stay confined to schools as it could be employed in faith groups, probation, youth offending teams, social care, in fact wherever there are young people who need support, guidance, and the wisdom of another person's hindsight.

Until organisations see the importance of mentoring and the role it can play in developing their staff, students or service users, they will lack the true strategic organizational mentoring opportunity; waiting to be utilized. For schools, this mentoring approach could also complement many of the national agendas that are desired as well as the quality kite marks i.e. Healthy Schools, Community Cohesion, Cultural Diversity Quality Standard (CDQS) or Parent Partnershipsjust to name a few. To solely use mentors for behaviour is a poor use of such a rich resource and is not a good return on investment. Put it this way, from just employing a few strategies you could get much more out of the provision than you already have and so could everyone else.

Marketing and branding is everything...

I really believe that everything I have ever done has come together during my career in education, which I feared would not have happened. One of the big things that I took from my music and event promotion days is the importance of marketing and branding. I realised quite quickly that within education mentoring had a bad name and was perceived derogatively by not only those within school but the wider community. I knew this had to be tackled head on and I had to work on changing the function, purpose and reputation of mentoring; to get the buy in from the staff, students and the parents. So that was the mission: create a programme that would be accepted by all and was viewed as professional and effective in how it was delivered. I started by working closely with the HoY as they would refer the pupils, due to their background knowledge of the students. I then provided a parental consent form that would highlight all the positive elements of mentoring and its promise that would be sent home.

During this time I also shared the successes, progress, new branding and launch of the RAMP mentoring programme via the whole school newsletter which raised its profile once again. I also shared the strategic vision of mentoring with the entire Senior Leadership Team in more than one SLT meeting, which I was given the opportunity to chair. I shared mentoring activities via the weekly pastoral meeting with the HoY's (I also became an Assistant Head of Year) and I presented to all the subject leaders at the Curriculum Leaders forum which I was a member of. So concerning all the different angles as a team we covered them and this enabled mentoring to have a very positive and high profile amongst the school community and also the parents in the wider community.

There is no 'I' in team

It was amazing, for we had changed the perception of mentoring within this school which was really a testament to hard work, commitment, heart and passion shown by the mentoring team. At the peak of mentoring within the school we had around 24 mentors which consisted of mentors from the community, the business sector (namely Ernst & Young), our local college and a core team within the school. This core team within the school was the secret to the effectiveness and productivity of the whole programme. The team consisted of Sandra Sterling who was my assistant and had bundles of mentoring wisdom, knowhow and was a tough cookie. Her savvy street knowledge and great insight into people as well as her soft and compassionate approach made her highly versatile and always in demand. Manjit Uppal, a passionate and loyal Liverpool supporter with a Liverpool mug to boot! Even though Manjit was so petite, looks can be very deceiving as she was a black belt in martial arts, a fitness fanatic who ran miles before the school day and also a football manager of our local Saturday league team. Manjit was truly effective and is one of the best mentors I have met. She has a way with all children and is very connected as she would at times shed a tear in some of the most distressing circumstances where children were affected by bad situations. We then had Adrian McCollin who was like a big bear but had a soft heart, when donning his infamous black coat - he could double for a security guard and when necessary his laid back demeanour would turn grizzly! Adrian loved working with young people and had a passion to connect with all children and had a crazy spin when it came to table tennis. Adrian was commonly effective in cases with some of the most challenging students that we never had success with, he had a good way and the team was well kitted. This was the team and we made a remarkable difference. On average between us, we delivered around 50-60 mentoring sessions on a weekly basis which was a great achievement, with Sandra & Manjit usually leading the way by mentoring students out of their ears and even parents on occasions.

"On average between us, we delivered around 50-60 mentoring sessions on a weekly basis."

From working in relative obscurity as a mentoring team to becoming an integral part of the school pastoral team, and ultimately impacting the academic aspects was no mean feat and not to be taken for granted. We enabled students to develop better relationships with their teachers and their peers as well as overcome their personal barriers to their learning. Mentoring had added a vital support mechanism to the lives of students, teachers and parents and our impact was undeniable and wholly recognised by the students.

From strength to strength!

We were now in a position where a broad range of pupils were even putting themselves forward to be mentored. We were being inundated with different pupils wanting to be mentored with the HoY increasing their mentoring requests and parents asking for us to support their children too. We then had a range of senior leaders frequently signposting and even bringing students to be mentored as a positive intervention and not just behavioural. The "various" mentoring programmes were now being viewed in a very positive light which helped the whole learning community to accept our work as whole school support for all. We mentored those who were gifted and talented, "the invisibles" and students who previously would not get a look in. The students and the learning community were now informed of what mentoring was and where students tried to manipulate the system i.e. coming when they felt like it or saying they were with the mentors when they were not were seriously reprimanded. So we cut out the negative aspects like students just turning up when they felt like it etc. This was previously a major annoyance to some teachers (and still is in some schools), who believed that we encouraged such behaviour which we never did. This is one of the reasons why I developed the whole school RAMP communication model. This model ensured the process for booking mentoring sessions was inclusive and transparent. By doing so, it enabled all teachers to receive notice of up and coming sessions via letters requesting their permission or emails, dependent on their preference. The purpose of this was to enable the teachers to be involved in the process and contribute to the sessions by sharing any pressing concerns they needed addressing. This really helped transform the relationship with the mentoring service and wider staff as this encouraged the teachers to feel they were a part of the magic. They could also make us aware when the students were having important lessons i.e. the start of course work, having tests or catch up lessons etc. so we could re-schedule the sessions. This enabled our approach to be less intrusive but complementary to the whole teaching and learning process.

Finally, teachers were more supportive and aware of the wider purposes of mentoring. They now understood that students were mentored for various reasons which were highlighted. All were now benefitting from a well rounded mentoring programme that was truly inclusive with a true every child matters ethos.

Be wise and strategize!

From the grassroots level of rolling up my sleeves and working with pupils from a variety of backgrounds who were faced with a variety of challenges, to then recruiting, interviewing, training and managing mentors from a range of careers, experiences and cultures. During this journey, I also became an Assistant Head of Year (AHoY). My role was to support the HoY to overlook the pastoral care of around 180 students. Also being a member of the Curriculum Leaders forum as the Director of Mentoring with the other heads of departments such as the Head of English, Head of Maths etc. and spending time on the Senior Leadership Team, my whole school knowledge was broad, unique, invaluable and strategic. I had now been exposed to what the students, teachers, community and parents needed. I was operating as an interpreter, translating broken English (Patois) street slang and street smarts into accessible language for all. It was all about fusing these elements together because one could not work without the other.

I recognised that there was a happy medium to be struck on a functional level for everyone to effectively collaborate. The RAMP® - Raising Achievement Mentoring Programme model added an extra dynamic that improved the whole school harmony and made us confident that whatever came we were now in a position to deal with it.

T Tips: 10 steps how to develop an award winning mentoring programme

1. Make sure the programme endorses holistic development of the learning community. This will be achieved by making the programme accessible to all.

2. Ensure that there is a significant Senior Leadership team buy in that is visible and this is communicated whole school via staff briefings, newsletters & home correspondence.

3. Make sure that your mentoring team is handpicked and multi-layered with a variety of staff ranging from senior to junior positions. This would give a breadth of quality, experience and credibility to the programme.

4. It is essential that your team is sufficiently trained and have the right skill sets to accommodate the variety of mentees who will be on the programme.

5. It is imperative to have a central point of the programme i.e. a coordinator or manager etc. who has a strategic role to ensure the programme is effectively delivered.

6. Make sure you have mentors who represent the local community or at least have a great insight into the challenges the community faces. This is important.

7. To document and evaluate the programme's quality, the right documentation and infrastructure needs to be in place so all mentors can sing off the same hymn sheet.

8. Create a positive buzz around the programme, re-launch, re-market, re-design do whatever it takes to get the desired outcome you want.

9. The best way to have more mentees is to have a strategic rolling programme.

10. Make sure there are incentives for those on the programme such as a rewards etc.

Encouragement Sweetens Labour

From humbling beginnings, personal and professional struggles to being accepted and recognised as a peer, professional practitioner and the respected Director of Mentoring. By no stretch of the imagination was this the easiest route as I went through football, business administration, music then education, but it has been well worth it. Now considered a beacon of hope for many young people still on their quest to discovering their identity, as they witnessed a young African Caribbean man not much older than 33 years old, now married with 3 daughters, who was respected by the community, pupils, school staff and parents who came from the streets but, was not confined to the streets.

"We were awarded the National School of the Year."

Due to the extensive work that we have done to address the disparity between "Black boy" underachievement we were awarded the "National School of the Year" by the National Black Boys Can organisation. I was called and made aware of the news whilst on paternity leave. I never attended the ceremony because I chose to stay with my baby Donna as we celebrated the birth our first daughter Serae. What was nice though, when I returned to work I was congratulated by Ken Morris the Head, and he gave me the trophy to house within my office which was a really nice gesture.

Small triangle cucumber sandwiches with no crusts

Due to the award and the recognition for our work we were then invited to the House of Lords. I was brought aside and asked to be a representative for the school by Ken so I accompanied the Deputy Head Sukhbir Farah. We entered this posh banqueting suite in the House of Lords right next to the River Thames. The suite was adorned with posh cutlery and exquisite fine china which we used to drink tea and as we ate cream cakes. In the midst of this extravagant scene, I was miles away in my own world reflecting on where I found myself and from where I had come. This was surreal and a far cry from living in a council flat without having enough money to turn the heating on. These two parallels were so conflicting, but I had lived both and now I was living the more favourable one.

At this juncture of my life I was experiencing the recognition for my work. I say my life's work because it took all that I had been through to be where I was. From being a volunteer mentor working with a handful of African Caribbean boys to overseeing a dynamic game changing mentoring programme with national recognition for being innovative and being the Director who governed its day to day operation. The mentoring of 5 students to our now turn over of approximately 160 mentees per academic year that covered all needs, the progression was significant.

Model School

On a visit to our school, the city wide mentoring coordinator after hearing of the work that we were doing, he stated that we were a "model school" for mentoring within the city. This was a great accolade as we grew from modest beginnings to develop mentoring into a meaningful support mechanism and now we were being recognised for it. We were also paid a visit by Elizabeth Reid who was the Chief Executive of the Specialist Schools and Academies Trust which was a big thing. On her visit she was escorted around to witness the school delivering its innovative curriculum and the good practice at Hamstead Hall. Due to being out for the day, it was organised that I would do an Oscar style pre-recorded presentation, for her to view in my absence. This was set up by Mr. Sneary who was the fitness man who ran a marathon or two! And was also the technology whiz who made it happen. The presentation went well and Elizabeth Reid watched it and afterwards expressed how impressed she was with our mentoring work and my view that Every Child Matters is the golden thread throughout any good school resonated with her.

"Every Child Matters is the golden thread throughout any good school."

It was our turn...

We received a call from Ofsted on the Friday and the visit was on the following Wednesday. Anyone who has been involved in a school that is about to undergo Ofsted would know about the pressure that would accompany these visits. It was all about new school displays, staff meetings and students being told to be on their best behaviour as they are representing the school. As a Director, I was told I would need to be in a meeting with 2 other senior figures: Ms Emson, who led on the wider care of the students and Miss Hoyte – who was one of the most militant teachers I have ever come across, even though she has mellowed down over time. I remember her hardcore demeanour as she would walk around the corridors in her boots that looked like something Gestapo officers would wear on their patrol. She was infamous for a short fuse and a sharpness of tongue which at first rubbed many up the wrong way. However, I can honestly say I have rarely met anyone in education who has such a genuine and authentic heart towards those within her care. She is someone that I could trust and her sincerity and deep devotion to serve children is rare in schools today. And what I respect about her is she's prepared to say it as it is and not mince her words while others prefer to pretty it up and gossip behind your back. That's not her style and I admire her for that.

The day of the meeting

During our meeting with the Ofsted inspectors, we were speaking about the pastoral care and well-being of the students. There were two inspectors who were serious and very straight to the point with their questions. There was one question that the female Ofsted inspector asked that remains with me even now. She asked, "How are the children doing spiritually?" that blew me away! At first, the question sounded more faith based than educational and since I never totally grasped the question's context I asked for clarification which she provided. She then asked a series of questions to prompt and give me a greater understanding, including: "How are the children's beliefs in themselves and their self-esteem? Are they confident in themselves? And does the mentoring work that you do impact on these aspects?" Now I got it, and it was right up my street! I went on to share what I view mentoring to be and how young people could be mentored without a negative behavioural history. I also shared that our mentoring programme was developed to raise aspirations and challenge underperformance by addressing areas of personal hindrance so they could flourish and holistically achieve their best. This went down well with the inspectors and when the inspection was done, I was told by my boss that they were highly impressed by my work and it was noted in the report. I was so glad to find out the areas on which our mentoring work directly impacted (Person development and Care, guidance

& support) were given grade 1, for outstanding! This was a whole school achievement and was a team effort, especially the work done by Kate Emson and Vivian Hoyte, amongst others. I would never attribute our mentoring work as being the main reasons for the school achieving these judgements, however I do recognise that our work added great value to the area of youth development and it made a significant impression on the inspectors who quoted the following in their report: "High quality provision for mentoring".

Opportunities lead to opportunities

After many years of work I was now being acknowledged and respected for my work. In the community I was now recognised as the 'go to' man concerning mentoring, as well as in the school and education world. I was also being given the opportunity to speak nationally at many high profile events, on how RAMP Mentoring could effectively engage BME students and raise their achievement. This was truly growing into my specialist area of authority and I educated senior leaders up and down the country on how they could get a better return on their mentoring investments. RAMP was working - it was validated by Ofsted; I was a visiting lecturer at the local college and a trainer of numerous mentors who desired to do the same.

I know where I am coming from

I have been privileged to experience success but I have not forgotten where I have come from. This would be foolish as it is still in me and gives me an edge in my field. I was brought up in Handsworth, which is within the inner city and from living in this rich and vibrant environment, which has given me eclectic experiences, I have been granted the opportunity to learn about people from various walks of life. This has been one of the most important factors when it comes to my ability to engage with young people who are currently going through their own "Handsworth" or inner city experience, whether their 'Handsworth' be in Hackney in London, Radford in Nottingham or St Pauls in Bristol. When you come from tough and challenging places you learn to understand frustration, desperation and discrimination from being misunderstood. It has cost me and there are many stories that are untold but, for this reason; I understand young people and do not find it a struggle or chore to connect with them. Whether they be black or white, they are never hard to reach. From what I have experienced, young people are REAL whether you like it or not and they have not yet learned the art of being politically correct, so what you see is what you get, which is too real for many. But I like it as I 'get' them and they 'get' me, so my work works.

> "Young people are REAL
> whether you like it or not."

The secrets

For this reason, I was given many opportunities to share my insight when it comes to engaging the "lost" or "hoodie" generation (as some would say). I believe my life has prepared me for this and I find it quite ironic that I now work within education when I was I was not the biggest fan of it, but now I am an advocate and have a healthy respect and appreciation for teaching and learning. I am now best positioned to help a generation of young people who are struggling to make sense of it all because for years I have had hundreds of one-to-one's, one to a few or group experiences and have listened to the thoughts, anxieties, frustrations, dreams and views of young people in the education system of our country. This has given me confidence and a great advantage when it comes to speaking on their behalf and articulating their experience.

Ernst & Young

As I have continuously stated, every child needs a mentor, even those who are considered 'bright'. These students may be considered to be your G&T (Gifted and Talented) who may be coasting and underperforming by doing just enough to get by. Hamstead Hall being a forward thinking school with Ken Morris at the helm was exploring the benefits of establishing a Business Education Partnership with Ernst & Young (E&Y) the accountancy firm and anyone who knows about accountancy will be aware that they are one of the big 4, which include Price Water Cooper, KMPG and Deloitte. So this was no small gig.

I was in the leadership meeting which was also attended by Juliet Bain who at the time was the National Manager for Corporate Social responsibility (CSR) at E&Y. At the meeting we discussed the possibilities and I shared my views that it would be a good match. From the meeting things went well. Ultimately, Hamstead Hall being one of the only schools nationally that E&Y would have a partnership with. I was responsible for training all their staff who were on the programme and what was impressive was E&Y had a great range of staff from national managers to high-end accountants who the company would charge out at up to £600 per hour to clients, so this was taken very seriously. I really enjoyed this project as it opened up my mind to other ways that I could add value to schools and private organisations via mentoring. This was a good education and business partnership which benefitted both E&Y and Hamstead Hall, so it was a win/win for everyone.

"It was still in my heart and something I was convicted to do."

So with the RAMP mentoring programme technology at full flow and at its height, I was overseeing approximately 24 mentors from school, community, college and the private sector. For an inner city school this was no small feat and this positioned our programme as one of the best mentoring programmes in the UK.

The pot was growing too small

Now due to developing my consultancy in the background, I was now attracting others who were interested in my work. I was at a point where I was now feeling that even though Hamstead Hall was the best place to be working, which had given me so much joy and many opportunities that I was grateful for, I still felt it was time to move on. This was a confusing time for me as it was the first real place I had worked for years and the school and people within it had given me so much. I would even well up with tears just thinking about giving a goodbye speech as the school and staff meant so much to me, not to mention saying goodbye to my mentee's, which was beyond comprehension and was even harder for me to do. However, even though I am man of sentiment, it was time to move on as it was my dream to work independently to replicate and provide mentoring programmes for schools up and down the country. In this way RAMP could help develop opportunities that would benefit schools and their students. I felt that even though I was not restricted by my boss and line manager - quite the opposite as they helped me so much - I was not able to truly experience my potential, whilst being in one school. What I had developed was highly transferable and so needed a national stage, but I really doubted leaving my job. I was the Director of Mentoring and the only one in the country; I was respected by my peers, had a respected position on the Curriculum Leaders forum and had tremendous influence within my school and city. I was also concerned about losing the holidays that you get in education, not to mention the big economic downturn as a result of the banks crashing and having been bailed out. We were now in the start of 2009, so what was I doing stepping out at that time? However, it was still in my heart and something I was convicted to do.

Walking on water...

It was time to leave. I was having the discussion with Donna and she was very supportive of my step to running my own business. She always supported me and saw my potential even when I didn't. I was encouraged by Donna's support which gave me a greater sense of urgency to move, but what could I do? I was also speaking to my mentors Karl George MBE, Michael Ekwulugo & Carlton Jones, who were preparing me mentally, emotionally, spiritually and financially. So with much advice, counsel, prayer and consideration; it was now time to move.

28 days to go...

It was time to resign! A resignation letter? I'd never written one, what do you do? I can remember the days when I was dying to get a job, and now I was on the verge of handing in my first ever resignation letter. How things had changed in my life. This was all new territory and each step was being taken like walking on an ice pond... tentatively! I remember when it was time to speak to my boss, it was challenging.

My boss was on his usual break duty commanding the stairs, ensuring there was no stampede to the food. I then made him aware I would like to have a word with him so he came to my office. When he entered my office it was as though he already knew what was coming, which was not easy for me. You see, Mr Kendrick Morris was truly a supporter, mentor and had became a dear friend as well as being my boss Under his reign he had seen me flourish and grow exponentially and for this I deeply respected him. He was a true leader with a desire for learning and never came across as un-teachable and he was always willing to learn. We would trade books, share insights and exchange our deepest desires to make a difference for young people. Even though he was my boss, he was secure enough to expose me to new opportunities that were outside of the organisation which would ultimately encourage my onward progression. He never ever stunted my growth, he was a mentor to me and always affirmed and encouraged me to know the value I had. I truly respect this man and he is still highly supportive of me and what I do. He is one of those innovative leaders that will continue to bring and welcome innovation into education delivery. He is a true gentleman and here I was about to tell him I was leaving! I felt like a traitor but I knew these were just feelings because of the fondness that I had for him. The letter was in my possession and there was no turning back. So I gave him the letter and he opened it. He then said something to the effect that he knew it was coming, but he shook my hand and he looked into my eyes with a look of being proud - the kind of look that a father would give to his beloved son. It was that moment when the time comes for the son to leave the family home as a young man. Ken had seen me grow from the ground up and he had played a significant part in my last stages. I knew he was proud of me; as my boss and an elder statesman. He accepted my resignation with such dignity and he released me with his blessing.

Time is ticking...

So I had just over 4 weeks to go which was all about succession planning with my team, saying goodbye to my mentees and fellow staff and preparing the way for my departure. There was one mentee that I found extremely hard to say goodbye to, as I was more than a mentor to him. I was like a big brother as his big brother, who I mentored previously, was in prison. It took a while to develop this relationship but now we understood each other. When it came time to share I was leaving he took it badly which made it harder, but he understood why and accepted it and he wished me well.

Time to give that goodbye speech

The day came when my departure was announced in our teachers' briefing. Ken shared a few kind words which were really touching. Then what happened next was unexpected… I never said anything! No departure speech, no one asked me to do one and I never volunteered. No tears which I thought were unavoidable because of how dear this phase was to my life, but I guess it was truly time to go. I have the deepest and fondest working memories of being at Hamstead Hall Community Learning Centre but now it felt like I had left home and I had to grow up quickly.

Right there under my nose

It was the Easter break and the date that I left work was Friday 3rd April 2009. It was strange; I now had to consider how to find work for myself. I had another school that I was working in part time that was soon to finish in May and I had an Academy who were interested in my services but I was pending a new CRB (which took 4 months until August to come through). So the reality of being self-employed was kicking in and this was all new to me, so even I had to watch this space.

Always have faith!

In May 2009, I was in London at a business meeting with a friend of mine Nathan Dennis. Whilst at this meeting, it was at the back of my mind that I was coming to the end of my other contract so I was soon to have no work, besides a bit of consultancy I was doing around the business and community engagement agenda with Nathan Dennis and Melissa Shervington of First Class Youth Direct. So in my new found freedom as my own boss I was having a board meeting by myself considering what was my next step which I needed to take quickly.

Whilst at this meeting, I received a call which was about to change everything. A Senior Education Advisor who would call me from time to time called me and left a message. I was now on the phone listening to this voicemail, when I heard the news that gave me sheer delight and a reason to punch the sky with excitement and relief. The message was to inform me that the city was going to deliver a mentoring programme to raise attainment and narrow the achievement gap and they wanted me to lead the project! Talk about a break through phone call! This call answered my faith and defined a benchmark in my journey as I was now truly on my way from leading mentoring in one school to leading mentoring in the second largest city in the United Kingdom!

Don't be scared to start again...

Just over 7 years ago, I began a new career as a volunteer mentor after making a bold decision to change my career at the age of 25 and start from scratch, which would be insane to many! I took the risk of turning my back on being a known recording artist to becoming an unknown mentor, which did pay off as I had now become the Lead Mentor in Birmingham city! This was an achievement in itself. My risk to change careers had paid off and the decision I made to walk and not stay at the music or school 'bus stops' turned out to be a good move.

"The city even adopted my RAMP brand as the name of the project."

New territory, new challenges

So for the next 2 years I was the Lead Mentor in Birmingham city, working within Primary and Secondary schools. My role was to deliver presentations to senior leaders, train their staff, manage the staff on the project, coach the mentors for CPD, develop the resources, deliver group sessions and motivational assemblies plus lead and further develop the city wide project. The city even adopted my RAMP name as the project name. This project proved that mentoring was more than a behaviour management strategy as the RAMP process was successfully transferred and implemented across the city. During this project, I received a Leading Aspect Award because my RAMP model closed the achievement gap, by improving pupil morale, well being and increased student performance and attainment.

How do you know that it works?

As an example, one of the schools that were involved in the citywide RAMP mentoring programme from the 26 year 11 students who were on the programme from their school, 14 out of the 26 went up a GCSE grade from an expected D to C! We also recorded the decrease of lateness, fixed term exclusions, poor attendance and E-portal logged incidents for negative behaviour. The RAMP programme has proved that once you cater for all parties everyone wins! The RAMP approach added value to how mentoring was perceived during the citywide project.

With countless delegates, mentees, teachers and senior leaders vouching for the programme's effectiveness, the RAMP mentoring model had now proven itself successful in a cross section of schools.

During this time, my work had empowered students, mentors and teachers and to read the evaluations and see the feedback was truly encouraging! What also blessed my heart was to hear the stories from the mentors I had worked with over the project. To hear how my input had encouraged them in their roles was rewarding. I was also given the opportunity and great privilege to train newly qualified teachers on their School Centred Initial Teacher Training (SCITT) on how to develop effective and meaningful relationships with their students via mentoring. This is a highlight on my calendar and career as I was now able to encourage, inform and equip the future educators who would impact young people in their classrooms across the country and ultimately the world. So from mentoring students to mentoring mentors, TA's, teachers and senior leaders was personally life changing, rewarding and simply beyond words.

Case Study:
Leading Aspect Award winning RAMP project   **CS**

Closing the achievement gap by effectively raising pupil morale, well-being, performance and attainment via The RAMP® - Raising Achievement Mentoring Programmes mentoring model.

Why this is leading practice

This unique mentoring programme has successfully engaged a wide range of students, staff and parents alike. By doing so, it has effectively improved pupil performance, promoted school and parental partnership, increased attainment as well as pupil well being. The RAMP® - Raising Achievement Mentoring Programmes model has been recognised as innovative by many within education and has been viewed as leading practise by Birmingham Local Authority.

Impact to date

Evidence that the students involved in this target group had raised their attainment was provided by case studies, questionnaires and core subject progress grades, for the period covered by the programme. They indicated that the target group had made progress in the following areas;

1. Attendance increased in some cases to 100%

2. E-portal computerized logged incidents reduced to zero

3. English and Maths grades improved by one full grade

4. Improvement in final GCSE grades

This had contributed to the increase in school wide results for 5A--C inz these subjects (27%--42%) and rising in all schools who participated on the project.

Interviews with pupils and staff supported the view that pupil morale and well-being had both been substantially raised by the programme. This was in part due to the achievements but also to the sense of purpose and the negotiation of personal targets. Evidence was presented to indicate that independent learning was now taking place and students were taking greater personal responsibility for their learning, relationships and academic attainment.

Rationale / Start Point

It was observed in the city that there was a gap in educational achievement between certain groups, for a variety of reasons. The aim of the RAMP programme was to narrow the gap in educational achievement, ensuring students from all ethnicities and cultures achieved their best.

It was identified that a strategic mentoring approach that not only helps students to be more focused, but also enabled them to overcome barriers such as academic, personal and social etc. It was found that mentoring could impact well-being as well as key indicators like GCSE grades, working at grades, attendance, punctuality and behaviour. And in doing so could achieve the city's objective to raise standards.

Key Strategies

The Key Strategies that have led to change are;

- Initial presentation made to senior leaders

- School based leading mentor appointed or identified from staff within school as a CPD opportunity

- Mentors trained, coached and given networking opportunities to promote good mentoring practise

- Innovative RAMP Academic Mentee Portfolio™ workbooks introduced to track and evidence pupil progress

- Mentoring and coaching identified as central to readiness to learn

- Emotional barriers to learning challenged

- ECM (Every Child Matters) agenda-bases for justification and rationale

- Bespoke individual training plans for target group

- Progress tracked and data analysed

- Parental involvement encouraged, facilitated and valued

Sustainability and Further Development

The success of the programme for the target group, its effect on the school as a whole and the way the mentoring programme has changed the learning environment, have led to ongoing senior staff endorsement and support. The RAMP mentoring programme, as a key element of CPD, has made a permanent change in staff approaches to learning encounters in the classroom and on a one to one basis. The intervention has sustainability and the model promotes strategic whole school delivery that embeds an aspirant mentoring culture within the learning community.

"I got choked up and was ready to cry."

Live the dream or die

This chapter of my life gave me great joy, relief, fulfilment and satisfaction. My dream of greatness was being realised. It's one of those 'Kodak' moments that I will never forget. When I was a youngster even though I came from challenging circumstances, a low income family, predominantly raised by a single mother in the inner city and not having the best academic ability, I still had a dream. I believed that I was born to be great and that greatness was within me. When I say this, I am not saying it in a boastful way, I just had an inner knowing that I was born for more than what I was experiencing or contributing to the world and it was something that I just could not let go of and it was not letting go of me. I shared this with some students in London during December 2011, who were discouraged and felt that they had no hope because of where they were living and the lack of opportunities in their area. I simply shared my heart and was so emotional I got choked up and was ready to cry and struggled to hold back the tears, because I believe that the only thing that is truly yours is your belief in yourself and your dream and you should never allow your circumstances, past, family, education or lack of it to take it away. Never lose hope as hope is life and a belief that things can change, that things can get better, that life can turn around and that one day things can be different. Never allow your past to dictate your future as you are more than you have experienced and you can be more than you imagine! I believe that there is greatness within everyone, it is just that some of us discover it ourselves and sometimes others discover it in us. That's why I believe every child needs a mentor to help them to discover their inner promise that at times is hidden.

In just over 7 years my life became virtually unrecognisable and I cannot take the credit for it. I did my part, I made my decisions, put my effort in and the benevolence of God helped me to do the rest. I also acknowledged I have been greatly helped by my supporters who have contributed to my success, for it has not been a solo effort as you will read on the dedication and acknowledgement pages in this book.

From starting out as a young boy in the inner city with a passion and talent for football, then a young man who entered the music industry as a recording artist to then ending up where I least expected to see myself, in education. From a volunteer to Director in 6 years within Hamstead Hall and a nationally recognised ambassador for mentoring; a business owner and the lead mentor of my city in a further 2 years. In less than 8 years I started out in a new career which would enrich lives in a way I could never imagine as well as my own, and to see the changes that were a result of my work. By my faith in Jesus Christ my life had changed and by my faith in people; I have helped many to change their lives so they could add value to their own communities, schools, families and themselves. I could not have had a more rewarding vocation even though it was one a fell into, or did I? My previous vulnerabilities, insecurities and weaknesses, now made others stronger! My past mistakes now offered a greater sense of direction to others, in a nutshell, my hindsight has become the foresight for many young people on similar life journeys, which is priceless.

If I could do it again, would I?

This has been a hard journey and at times I have felt that life has taken more from me than it has given me. Some challenges have been unbearable but some have been due to me making my decisions or not making my decisions, most of my pain to be brutally honest has been self inflicted (that's me taking personal responsibility). On reflection, would I have changed my decisions? Would I have done anything different? If possible, would I have avoided some of the pain that I have endured? These are questions that I would ask myself but to tell the truth, however painful, distressing, challenging and stretching the journey has been, I would go through it again. Because how would I have known how to express myself without those 10,000 hours of writing, thinking, rehearsing and introspecting. How would I have been able to address auditoriums of school leaders publically without those hours of practise in front of the mirror with a torch in my hand?

How could I advise a potential football protégé about not placing all his eggs in one basket and depending on their head not just his legs with such conviction without me doing the opposite? How would I be able to understand the pain of some of my mentees and their distresses at life's turns without experiencing some of those turns myself? You see, the richness of my soul's tapestry is the embroidery of a life well lived, the University of Life well attended as well as a mind that has been to the brink, looked over and come back. My pain has now birthed my pleasure and is now a comfort for me and many who needed to see that life can turn around for the better; and the failures of the past and the failures of their pasts don't have to dictate the successes of their future.

In reflection, it was never easy but anything worth doing is always hard. For this reason, depth of character is essential as resilience is one of those qualities that are only developed under trial. In the same way as muscles are developed by resistance and diamonds are only formed under pressure. So I encourage you to accept that most of the accomplishments you desire to achieve will, rarely be achieved without the experience of personal difficulties and challenges. But you can make it and you must, as someone's life is depending on you to make your break through! Dig deep into your inner reserve of strength for you have great inner treasure, so accepting anything less is self robbery. I have personally learnt at great cost that ALL things can work for your good just like it says in the bible, so no life experiences are ever wasted, whether they are good or bad, as long as you learn from them. So please live your purpose on purpose, for that's the reason why you were born. Herman Stewart.

"It was never easy but anything worth doing is always hard."

Personal Reflection:

1. What 5 things do you consider to be your best achievements?

2. Within your life what are the 3 major things that you would like to experience?

3. When was the last time that you really voiced your appreciation to someone who has done a lot for you in life?

4. Write down how you last felt when you were appreciated. Why not return that feeling to someone else.

The Future of Mentoring - Success School

Genesis

It all started in this session... whilst walking around in this high tech classroom similar to a James Bond scene, something dawned on me... many young people have a very clear vision in their hearts and minds of what they want to have and what they want to be! But many do not have the map or directions of how to get to that place and that's why every child needs a mentor. This was such a touching revelation because at first, I never saw it that way; at least it was not as tangible.

I was working with some pupils who were a few months away from taking their final GCSE exams. These pupils were meant to be bright and they were, but while I was delivering these sessions to them I was sensing a great apathy. Even though these pupils were the hope of their school, as I was in the company of some who were promised A*s and were academically gifted, there was a lack of something, a spark, a motivation, in fact a sense of purpose! From speaking further with them, I discovered the reason for the apathy I was sensing and this is an epidemic in education and experienced by many regardless of their ability. As our conversations started to develop, I discovered that the majority of students never had any passion for school or education, even though they were bright and able. As these students started to share with me, their paradox was very intriguing. The reason for my fascination was I always had such conversations with those who found school and the demand of scholastic education hard and too demanding, but this was a different kettle of fish. I now found myself coaching bright students with some having the potential to achieve the highest GCSE grades. But what was about to become crystal clear to me, was about to change my life and the lives of many young people in their generation.

Knowing the why, makes the how easier

As they started to share with me their disgruntlement and views of a practice the school used to motivate them (their achievement levels were placed on public display for all students to see!) which they felt wasn't right. After hearing their gripes, I could see where they were coming from as it could negatively affect the morale and self esteem of some students. They were sharing with me the kind of approaches that were being used, which after hearing I do agree borderline on negligence of student emotional and mental care. They then went on to share what the crux of the matter was for them. This was truly an education in itself and the most gourmet food for thought. What they then shared was... they did not get it! Basically they could not see a deep, congruent and personal point to school, education and its purpose and some who were present were not clear concerning where they were going in life itself. This was concerning, very concerning for two reasons. Here we had students who were deemed as highly academic, astute and gifted. At the same time, they were coming to the end of their compulsory education and yet they just confessed that they do not get it! I could see that they needed some serious guidance, encouragement and clarity. They needed a mentor, and here I was for the next couple of weeks.

"Aspirant Mentoring is important."

The spark...

During one of our following sessions, I had a eureka moment that would potentially fill this knowledge gap that was expressed by these students. This eureka moment was the birthing of the vision "Success School". With this group I decided to do a success visualization activity to help them to identify, explore and articulate what success meant to them personally. So I gave the students a piece of A4 paper each and a task that was about to change everything! At least the results of the task changed my previous approaches to youth engagement. This was paradigm shifting stuff.

So the students had their piece of paper and I gave them the following instructions: "I want you to draw a picture of what success looks like to you. You do not need to be an artist and the pictures do not need to be perfect. Just draw to the best of your ability and that should be fine". In response they all looked at me, some with a smile and some with bewilderment, but they all responded with nods or verbal gestures to express "ok" and they started to draw. In the room there was then a quiet excitement, a creative tranquillity as these young and impressionable students started to share what they perceived their personal successes looked like. Some of the pictures could be considered credible pieces of art, while some of the students just sketched bubble and stick figures. As I walked around and viewed their drawings of success, I was then illuminated with my own Edison light bulb moment. In a sheer moment of inspiration from above like the apple on Newtown's head came "Success School"- teaching young people how to be successful! I honestly cannot take credit for this, as it was so instant and without cognitive effort. But once it came I was immediately filled with the feeling of 'eureka!'. The moment was then extended as I further realised in the twinkling of an eye, that even though schools teach children subjects such as English, Maths, Geography and Biology etc. schools do not teach students about themselves, who they are, how to discover their dreams or how to become "successful" according to their personal attributes and aspirations. For this reason "Aspirant Mentoring" is important.

True success is personal

As we came back together, I asked all of the students to share their picture and an explanation of what they had drawn. As they stood one by one and shared, you could see them lighting up with excitement. Just to see their faces as they shared their dreams of success and to be listened to, validated and applauded by their class mates was truly rewarding. One student shared how he would like to become successful by using his heart to make music, write books and influence the world by his thoughts. Another shared how she would like to work in New York as a journalist with an office in a place similar to the Empire State Building. She went on to share she would like to live in a 3 story town house and have 3 children with the eldest and youngest being boys and the middle one a girl. She then shared she would also like to have a husband and live on a farm doing agriculture with her family as she would like to experience both the city and country way of living. Then one of her peers expressed that he would like to become successful and wealthy so he could be a philanthropist and give a lot of his money away to help people. Student after student shared their pictures of success which was truly inspiring! How they shared them was so articulate and bold as they became vulnerable enough to share what was on the inside and meant a lot to them.

"Their 'why' would put education into context."

This experience truly touched me and I then knew that Success School was something I had to develop because of what I experienced in this room plus, a) This was something that children desperately needed, but would seldom receive within a formal classroom setting and b) This was a major missing link that would change how children achieve and experience personal development. Success School would now provide a forum that would enable young people to get in tune with who they really are and their passions which would become their personal source of inspiration. In turn this would dramatically accelerate their personal, social and academic development because they would be clear on their "why" which would put education into context.

The horse and the cart

I have heard this expression many times before concerning the cart going before the horse and in my experience; it has never been a positive analogy. In real life, no one would dare put the cart before the horse as there would be a lot of confusion paired with no movement! The horse is always meant to go before the cart for both to move forward. In this example the horse is the child's passions, dreams or aspirations and the cart is education or the other vehicles that can help the child to follow their dreams. If we view it in this way, it makes total sense why many children do not achieve anywhere near their inherent potential. It is like asking someone who loves swimming the breast stroke to pursue playing the cello or a passionate javelin thrower to enthusiastically pursue a career in show jumping. This is what is done when we expect students to be enthusiastic about getting 5 GCSEs including English and Maths in school, regardless of their talents, passions and strengths. Somehow it just doesn't seem logical or fair but this is how the education system works at present. For best results, aspirations and passion must be identified or explored to enable true achievement to be attained. This approach is the opposite of how the education system motivates students to achieve their best. Sadly, schools put the cart (education) before the horse (the child's passion or aspiration) and this is one of the main reasons why children become disenfranchised and have no further interest in education after they have done their compulsory time. Many then leave school to find themselves.

5 tips of how to get the best out of young people

1. Don't force them, learning is not passive so if they do not want to learn they won't in those instances. Gently coax them into seeing the benefit for themselves to engage.

2. Where possible, make their aspirations relevant to what they are doing in the curriculum. If they want to run a business, make the relevance to tax and overheads with Maths etc. they must see the why as it then makes the how easier.

3. Work specifically in collaboration with the parent or Carer that the student has a healthy reverence / fear of. Over the years I have learnt to connect with the parent that the child would prefer me not to so this works as a deterrent which encourages increased engagement.

4. Develop a healthy relationship that transcends simply being their educator. Pupils are people first and if you engage them as a person they would see that you have a sincere care for them.

5. Never be above saying sorry. Humility is lacking in schools as many members of staff will not admit they are wrong. This is one of the easiest ways to lose the respect of students. So if you're wrong just say sorry, if you over react say you did or if you shouted unnecessarily just admit it. It will gain their respect and engagement. This is easier said than done but, is well worth the rewards.

You need something personal

In my years of transforming the educational experience of students, so they become passionate about their own learning, it has been less of the outside in, but more of the inside out approach. You do not need to look far to see those who really achieve in life, business, sports, politics, law or music etc. they do it in the 'passion first' order. First conviction, second competence, thirdly results. Look at those who have achieved great feats - it is because their motivation, passion and drive have come from the inside and a conviction that compelled them to achieve something of meaning to them and then the wider world. When you look at Martin Luther King Jr., Helen Keller, Thomas Edison, Bill Gates, Michael Jordon Jr., Mahatma Ghandi and Michael Jackson, they all achieved great feats in different times, fields and industries but one thing they all had in common was passion, vision and ability. Not all had a great scholastic education but notably some did, for example Ghandi was a solicitor and Martin Luther King Jr had a doctorate, but others even dropped out of formal education such as Bill Gates, Sir Richard Branson and the late Steve Jobs who have achieved their dreams and what success means to them. They have also established some of the biggest companies in the world. So how come we're getting it so wrong?

I have a dream! But what is it?

For anyone to achieve anything that demands a lot of sacrifice, commitment and dedication, they really need to understand their own why. Why am doing it? Why would it be beneficial? Why do I have to do it this way? And this would be no different for young people within schools, colleges and universities. Could this be the reason why so many children drop out and get categorised as NEET? (Not in Employment Education or Training) and being disengaged? Is it because they do not know why? I know there is more to it than that, but in the cake I can bet just like the flour in a cake is the main ingredient, the lack of a 'meaningful why' is also a main ingredient in the cake of student disenfranchisement. I would go as far as saying many have not been helped to discover or been exposed to activities that could prompt their meaningful why out of them. Some may say this is not the purpose of education, but I would disagree. The word "education" was derived from the word "educe" which was first mentioned in around 1600s and it means to: "bring out or draw out something hidden such as latent potential" (slightly paraphrased but the meaning is accurate). So to educate should be to get something out of someone, namely their potential. So if this is what education does I am all for it, but when education is just focussed on filling young people with predominantly academic notions I believe it truly falls short of educating.

"What is in it for me?"

Inner incentive, external results.

The reason I have mentioned the above is when I work with some of the most disenfranchised students or those who do not engage with school, I have had to open their eyes so they can see their own benefit for doing well and one that resonates with them. For someone to want to achieve they must see the "What is in it for me?" element. I do not mean it in a self-absorbed and narcissistic sense, but in a personally engaging way, because even someone who is a humanitarian does it partly because it satisfies them to be altruistic. So even the most selfless person must have an inner incentive why they do what they do (for Ghandi it was the liberation of India from its colonial masters) then where possible we can help children to experience their own reason for their passion or contribution to their own success, we must help them identify what it is for them so they can move towards it. For years this has been one of the most significant reasons I have experienced success with children, because I have helped them to experience their own eureka moments by connecting them with their own passions and possibilities.

Activity:

1. If you were to draw a picture of success what would it look like? Please describe it?

2. When you get a chance, ask your child, a niece, cousin or younger sibling to do the same.

3. When you were a child, what did success look like to you? Have you exceeded that picture, given it up or still working on it?

Shouldn't they know though?

In many respects they should know the importance and relevance of school, but the reality is many do not and it is a great hindrance. But let us explore this further as it does make perfect sense... Let's take it from their view. Let's create two characters: Sharon and Pete. Sharon and Pete both enter the school system at the age of 4 years old and both go to reception school. This is their entry point into the world of education and they are both too young to truly understand what they are signing up to, plus they don't sign up to it; their parents do. So they both just accept that they have to go to school. Before their introduction there may be limited discussion concerning what is about to happen and due to their age, any explanation would not be highly descriptive. So both go to school and it becomes habit. Both Sharon and Pete like school for similar reasons; they both like the work and their friends even though at times they don't feel like going to school. Infant school and Primary school shortly follows and they are now both more aware of school and why they need to attend. They then complete Primary school learning, where most of their lessons were delivered by one teacher and is pretty much centred around relationships where they feel safe and within a group of peers that they are always around. Now it is time to leave Primary school as they get ready for Secondary education.

> "They now have around 15 teachers who teach them one subject each."

As they go to Secondary school, they now have to navigate around the big school building and have to come to terms with being the smallest in the school when they were just the tallest in Primary school! Instead of the one teacher they had, who taught them pretty much everything, they now have around 15 teachers who teach them one subject each. There is now a new bunch of expectations that they never had before i.e. intense assessment, discipline and detentions for being late etc. for many this experience is truly overwhelming and some lose their way because their transition was not properly facilitated or they were not informed as much as they could have been, in relation to the level of change they were to encounter. Pete adapts well and conforms to the new regime, and is enjoying school and what it throws at him.

In this transition of a few years from 11 to 16 some gain a personal epiphany of why they are in school and then are internally aware and motivated to delve deeper to know at least what industry they want to work in or some have a clear vision concerning where they want to go. On the other hand, Sharon does not adjust well and does not enjoy the experience. She also lacks the personal epiphany and cannot wait to leave school and does not plan to go there again!

Is it my fault that I don't get it all?

Those who know usually do well or have a better chance of experiencing success in school. They will have mentoring via an attentive parent, older sibling, family friends or role models who they have modelled their context of life from. In this phase of life when decisions are being made, ideas formed and paths chosen is when every child needs a mentor. I cannot tell you how much I have appreciated my mentors who have helped me to come to a decision in an area that I am not knowledgeable in because of their knowledge. That is why mentoring must be at least accessible to all children even if they do not use it. The schools and youth centred organisations of the future are going to be those who are not rigid but innovative in their approach to improve the potential of those in their care namely by mentoring.

One size does not fit all so school as an experience, is not exhilarating for some whilst it is for others. I believe the government could do much more to creatively communicate "The Big Why!" in a relevant way. More children would enjoy their school lives which would result in so much more all round success. This is why I developed Success School! To help young people discover their passions, by having a personal epiphany and discover their big why. I believe, if they understood the "why" the how becomes easier! This is where Success School comes in. Success School helps young people to achieve their potential by firmly placing the horse (passion and aspirations) in front of the cart (school and grades).

"There needs to be education about education!"

Students really need relevant education about the need for education!

From my findings I have found that there needs to be education about education! This is so taken for granted. I am not dismissive or gullible, but the reality of it is a lot of children don't get it! And we can help them to get it if we provide opportunities that will open their eyes by providing quality mentoring for them and enabling our hindsight to become their foresight.

This was the beginning of "Success School". To be continued...

Our Greatest Fear - Marianne Williamson

Our deepest fear is not that we are inadequate.
Our deepest fear is that we are powerful beyond measure.

It is our light not our darkness that most frightens us.

We ask ourselves, who am I to be brilliant, gorgeous,
talented and fabulous?

Actually, who are you not to be?
You are a child of God.

Your playing small does not serve the world.

There's nothing enlightened about shrinking so that other people
won't feel insecure around you.

We were born to make manifest the glory of God that is within us.

It's not just in some of us; it's in everyone.
And as we let our own light shine,
we unconsciously give other people
permission to do the same.

As we are liberated from our own fear, Our presence
automatically liberates others.

—Marianne Williamson

About the Author

Herman's rise to prominence may have developed rapidly, but the people closest to him would tell you he was never a novice at infusing hope and direction to his family, friends and peers.

Aspirations to be great started to materialise; the first of many adventures becoming a successful football player, with Great Britain's Under 15 football team, rubbing shoulders with stars like Manchester United's Paul Scholes.

Further on, Herman's creative ability turned to music. The Pioneer of an urban music collective he shared the stage with international superstars like Busta Rhymes, Wu Tang Clan and Redman; gaining him international acclaim. He also appeared on the ever popular Radio 1 with Tim Westwood, Choice FM with 279 and Galaxy FM. He also starred in a music video aired on MTV.

Always the entrepreneur, Herman was destined for success but not as he thought. On the verge of signing a contract for a Sony record label he had a change of heart. It might seem crazy but Herman knew this was not what he really wanted: the professional music career, football and dreams of stardom subsided; a new avenue was about to open and it was called Mentoring.

Assessing the big picture he accepted the challenge to encourage others and has not looked back. From volunteer Mentor to the Lead Mentor of his city and now a consultant, author, trainer and speaker in high demand, addressing and speaking to Senior Leaders and similar professionals within the Public and Private sector and a revered role model among young people within his vast area of influence.

Yet in the midst of all his achievements he retracts to remember the less fortunate and the road he could have taken, by visiting incarcerated offenders both young and old to share his story and why they should never give up.

The once self-proclaimed perfectionist has turned the spotlight from himself on to others by using his gifts to successfully equip and develop the current generation. Passionate, and non-pretentious, Herman's life experience makes his story rich with depth, welcomed and honoured by all people, from the young child, to the elders of society – in a nutshell the 'Professional person and People's man'.

Diagram 1.1

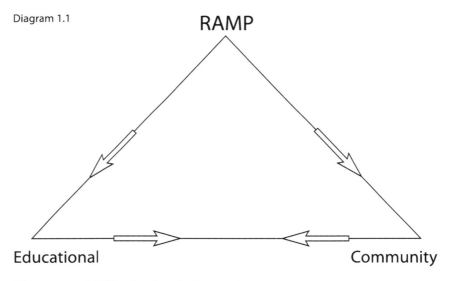

If you would like further information on our:

- Award winning RAMP - Raising Achievement Mentoring Programmes

- RAMP Staff Training

- Motivational Assemblies

- RAMP Consultancy

Please email: enq@rampmentoring.com

For further information please visit: www.rampmentoring.com

Printed in Great Britain
by Amazon.co.uk, Ltd.,
Marston Gate.